COMPARING ELECTORAL SYSTEMS

CONTEMPORARY POLITICAL STUDIES SERIES

Series Editor: John Benyon, *University of Leicester*

A series which provides authoritative and concise introductory accounts of key topics in contemporary political studies.

DAVID BROUGHTON
Public Opinion and Political Polling in Britain

MICHAEL CONNOLLY
Politics and Policy Making in Northern Ireland

DAVID FARRELL
Comparing Electoral Systems*

JUSTIN FISHER
British Political Parties*

ROBERT GARNER
Environmental Politics*

WYN GRANT
Pressure Groups, Politics and Democracy in Britain*

WYN GRANT
The Politics of Economic Policy

DEREK HEATER AND GEOFFREY BERRIDGE
Introduction to International Politics

ROBERT LEACH
British Political Ideologies

PETER MADGWICK
British Government: The Central Executive Territory

PETER MADGWICK AND DIANA WOODHOUSE
The Law and Politics of the UK Constitution

PHILIP NORTON
Does Parliament matter?

MALCOLM PUNNETT
Selecting the Party leader

ROBERT PYPER
The British Civil Service*

* Available from Macmillan Press from 1 January 1999 and from Prentice Hall Europe until then

COMPARING ELECTORAL SYSTEMS

DAVID M. FARRELL

MACMILLAN

First published by
Prentice Hall/Harvester Wheatsheaf
Hemel Hempstead, Hertfordshire

Published 1998 by
MACMILLAN PRESS LTD
Houndmills, Basingstoke, Hampshire RG21 6XS
and London
Companies and representatives
throughout the world

ISBN 0–333–75468–9

A catalogue record for this book is available
from the British Library.

This book is printed on paper suitable for recycling and
made from fully managed and sustained forest sources.

10   9   8   7   6   5   4   3   2   1
07   06   05   04   03   02   01   00   99   98

Printed in Great Britain by
Antony Rowe Ltd
Chippenham, Wiltshire

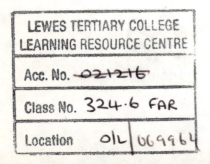

CONTENTS

TABLES AND FIGURES

Tables

Figures

PREFACE AND ACKNOWLEDGEMENTS

Electoral systems are currently much in vogue, in the new democracies, more than a few of the established democracies, and among the small but growing group of academic scholars specializing in this area. Having long been a relatively stagnant and unchanging field, it has now assumed a position of importance and attracted great interest. For some time Douglas Rae's seminal *The Political Consequences of Electoral Laws* (1967) stood alone. In recent years we have seen a number of important studies, such as Rein Taagepera and Matthew Soberg Shugart's *Seats and Votes* (1989), and Arend Lijphart's *Electoral Systems and Party Systems* (1994), to mention but a few. Suddenly, a lot more people are analysing electoral systems and their political consequences. This book aims at making this research more accessible to the lay and undergraduate audience.

In the researching and drafting of early chapters I benefited greatly from a period at the University of New South Wales, Canberra in early 1994. I am heavily indebted to Ian McAllister for having made this fellowship possible. While at Canberra I was extremely fortunate to meet Malcolm Mackerras from whom I learned a great deal about the quirks of Australian electoral systems. The book was completed in Manchester, and if I can be thankful for just one thing about the current peripatetic lifestyle of my partner, Arlene McCarthy, it is that she was not around much to distract me!

The following colleagues were very helpful in providing advice and information: Luciano Bardi, Shaun Bowler, David Broughton,

Yoram Gorlizki, Paul Harris, Sergei Kondrashov and Thomas Poguntke. I also wish to express my thanks to: J. P. Pomeroy of the Australian Electoral Commission, Christopher Siddall of the International Foundation for Electoral Systems, Elizabeth Winship of the Office for Democratic Institutions and Human Rights at the Conference on Security and Cooperation in Europe, Arend Lijphart who gave me access to his data on proportionality and party system characteristics, and Paul Wilder of the Arthur McDougall Fund who proved to be an invaluable source for advice and information. When Clare Grist of Prentice Hall/Harvester Wheatsheaf first approached me with the idea of writing this book I am sure she never realized how long it would take to complete! I thank her for her forbearance, and for her gentle bullying and cajoling. I am also grateful to Ruth Pratten and Ian MacQuarrie for having shepherded this through its closing stages. I want to record a special thanks to my readers, David Denver and Richard S. Katz, whose comprehensive, detailed and very encouraging comments greatly assisted the final drafting. Of course, any errors or omissions which remain are entirely my own.

My interest in electoral systems was first kindled in the early 1980s by reading Enid Lakeman's *How Democracies Vote* (the 1970 edition). I was fortunate to meet Enid on a few occasions. Her energetic, enthusiastic and encyclopaedic interest in electoral systems was contagious, and her untimely death in 1995 was a great loss. This book is dedicated to her memory.

D.M.F.
Manchester, March 1996

I

THE STUDY OF ELECTORAL SYSTEMS

1.1 Why study electoral systems?

For people who do not specialize in this area, electoral systems are usually seen as a big 'turn-off'. It can be difficult to instil much interest in the subject of counting rules; to enthuse about the details of how one electoral system varies from another. After all, how many wars were fought over whether the electoral formula was 'largest remainder' or 'highest average'? How many politicians have been assassinated over the issue of 'single transferable vote' (STV) *versus* 'first past the post' (FPTP)? Pity the student on a hot Friday afternoon who has to struggle through the niceties of the 'Droop quota'! Pity the teacher who has to burn midnight oil getting to grips with the issue of 'monotonicity'! It does seem fair to pose the question: why bother? What is the point of spending time examining electoral systems?

Several reasons can be given. First, a very large and growing number of people specialize in electoral systems, so *somebody* must think these systems are important! In the 1989 edition of his *International Bibliography on Electoral Systems*, Richard S. Katz (1989) listed some 1,500 works 'dealing with the forms and effects of representation and electoral systems'. By 1992 this list had grown to 2,500 works (Katz, 1992). Among these some have made significant developments in the methodology of studying electoral systems. For over twenty years one name has predominated in all textbook treatments of electoral systems. The seminal work by Douglas Rae (1967) set the trend on how to study electoral systems and their political consequences. It is only in the past five years or so that Rae's work has come under closer scrutiny as scholars, like Michael Gallagher, Richard Katz, Arend Lijphart, Matthew Shugart and Rein Taagepera, have sought to develop and improve on some of his ideas. Their work (and the work of others) needs to be incorporated into the textbook treatment of electoral systems. This is one of the major functions of this book.

Second, electoral systems are worth examining because they have become politically interesting. With the process of democratization, first in Mediterranean Europe in the 1970s, and then more dramatically in central and eastern Europe at the end of the 1980s, important decisions had to be taken on which electoral systems to adopt in the fledgling representative democracies. As we shall see in later chapters, in none of these cases was the 'British' system of 'FPTP' chosen; in only one case (and only briefly) was the STV system selected. It is interesting to speculate on the reasoning behind these particular decisions. Of even greater interest is the recent trend towards *reform* of existing electoral systems, notably in Italy, Japan and New Zealand – all within the past three to four years. This contradicts the impression that electoral reform is rare, only occurring 'in extraordinary historical situations' (Nohlen, 1984: 218). These reforms also give evidence to a growing sympathy for the 'German' two-vote (often referred to as the 'additional member') electoral system, as we see in chapter 5. Suddenly electoral reform looks possible, not just some theoretical notion of unrealistic, out of touch academics.

There is a third reason why it is important to study electoral systems and that is because they define how the political system will function. Metaphorically, electoral systems are the cogs which keep the wheels of democracy properly functioning. In almost any course on politics the following themes generally feature as important topics for consideration: elections and representation; parties and party systems; government formation and the politics of coalitions. In each of these areas, the electoral system plays a key role. Depending on how the system is designed it may be easier or harder for particular politicians to win seats, or for particular parties to gain representation in parliament, and it may be more or less likely that one party can form a government on its own. In short, there are important questions about the functioning of political systems which are influenced, at least in part, by the design of the electoral system.

Apart from their primary function of ensuring the smooth running and accepted legitimacy of the system, electoral systems are designed to fulfil a number of other – often conflicting – functions, such as reflecting the wishes of voters, producing strong and stable governments, electing qualified representatives, and so on. In selecting a particular design of electoral system, the 'electoral engineers' have to take important decisions about which function to stress most. As a result, no two countries have the same electoral system.

1.2 Electoral laws and electoral systems

It is important to distinguish between electoral *laws* and electoral *systems*. Electoral laws are the family of rules governing the process of elections: from the calling of the election, through the stages of candidate nomination, party campaigning and voting, and right up to the stage of counting votes and determining the actual election result. There can be any number of rules governing how to run an election. For instance, there are laws on who can vote (citizens, residents, people over seventeen years of age, the financially solvent, etc.); there can even be laws, such as in Australia or Belgium, obliging citizens to turn out to vote. Then there are usually a set of rules setting down the procedures for candidate nomination (e.g. a minimum number of signatures, a deposit). The campaign process can also be subject to a number of rules: whether polling, television advertising or the use of campaign cars is permitted; the size of billboards; the location of posters; balance in broadcasting coverage, and so on.

Among this panoply of electoral laws there is one set of rules which deal with the process of election itself: how citizens vote, the style of the ballot paper, the method of counting, and the final determination of who is elected. It is this aspect of electoral laws with which this book is concerned. This is the electoral system, the mechanism of determining victors and losers, which clicks into action once the campaign has ended. This is the stage where the political pundits take over from the politicians; where the television companies dust off their 'pendulums' and 'swingometers' and wheel out their latest computer graphic wizardry. Campaign slogans and electoral recriminations have ended. All attention is focused on thousands of people shuffling ballot papers in 'counting centres' throughout the country. (At least, this is the situation in Britain. In other countries,

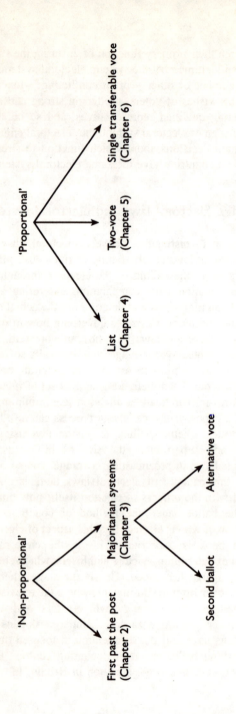

Figure 1.1 The five main types of electoral systems.

the counting and even the voting are done by computer.) Politicians, journalists and (some) voters wait with baited breath for the returning officer to announce 'the result'. TV presenters work long into the night, probing with their panelists the meaning of the results and assessing the voters' 'verdict'.

This scenario of 'election night coverage' is common to most political systems. There may be some variation in detail, but the basic theme is similar: we the voters have voted, and now we are waiting to see the result of our votes, in terms of who wins or loses and in terms of the number of seats won by each of the parties. It is the function of the electoral system to work this transformation of votes into seats. To put this in the form of a definition: *electoral systems determine the means by which votes are translated into seats in the process of electing politicians into office.*

Exactly how this translation occurs varies from one system to the next. In some systems great effort is made to ensure that the number of seats each party wins reflects as closely as possible the number of votes it has received. In other systems greater importance is attached to ensuring that one party has a clear majority of seats over its competitors, thereby (hopefully) increasing the prospect of strong and stable government. The first of these systems is said to be 'proportional', in contrast to the others which are 'non-proportional' electoral systems.

This book deals with the five main types of electoral system currently in use (Figure 1.1). First, there are the two more common forms of non-proportional systems, FPTP and the variants of majoritarian systems (alternative vote and second ballot). The distinguishing feature these systems share is that they do not aim at a proportional result; instead, far more attention is paid to the question of governmental stability and – generally being based on single-member constituencies – to notions of constituency representation. By contrast, the far more common family of proportional systems do aim specifically at achieving degrees of proportionality in the electoral result, although with mixed success, as we shall see. Chapters 2–6 deal with the operation of each of the systems in turn, describing how the system works, how it has adapted (if at all), and the political context in which it has operated. Having dealt with each of the systems in some detail, the book concludes, in chapter 7, with an assessment of the political consequences of electoral systems, dealing with such questions as: proportionality vs. stability; the role of representatives; party campaigns, and the potential for strategic voting.

As pointed out earlier, central to any discussion about electoral systems and their reform are questions of stability and the representation of minority interests. One is often seen as, at least partially, a trade-off against the other. A main contention of this book is that this argument is fallacious: that an electoral system can allow for maximum representation of minority interests without necessarily threatening the stability of government. We will return to this point in the concluding chapter, having reviewed the comparative evidence in chapters 2–6.

Before proceeding to an analysis of the different electoral systems, it is necessary to deal with two issues central to the study of electoral systems: (1) the issue of representation, and (2) the attempts to, as it were, 'artificially' influence the effects of electoral systems.

1.3 Conflicting views on the meaning of 'representation'

The precise meaning of the term 'representation' can vary markedly. The basic distinction is between a 'microcosm' and a 'principal-agent' conception of representation (McLean, 1991; Reeve and Ware, 1992). The first of these is associated with proponents of proportional electoral systems, the second with supporters of non-proportional systems. A classical exponent of the microcosm view was John Adams, one of the founding fathers of the USA, who said that parliament 'should be an exact portrait, in miniature, of the people at large, as it should think, feel, reason, and act like them' (quoted in McLean, 1991: 173). Taken literally this perspective is similar to the governing principle behind public opinion polls, i.e. the notion of a representative sample. In other words a society which is made up of distinct sets of ratios (e.g. men:women 50:50; urban:rural 70:30; middle class:working class 40:60; black:white 20:80), should elect a parliament which reflects these ratios in microcosm. To put it another way, parliament should be a 'representative sample' of the population. Obviously it is impossible to achieve a perfect representative sample, but the aim should be to get as close as possible to it. On this view, as Lord Plant (1991: 16) explains, 'the representativeness of a parliament is accounted for by its proportionality'. It is a sociological mirroring of society.

According to the microcosm conception of representation, there-fore, it is the pattern of composition of the parliament that matters, but, according to the principal-agent conception, it is the decisions of the parliament that matter. The basis of the principal-agent concep-tion is the notion of one person acting on behalf of another. The representative is elected by the people to represent their interests. In this case, even if the parliament is comprised of a preponderance of fifty-year-old, white, middle-class males, it is representative provid-ing it is seen to be taking decisions on behalf of the voters. It is less important that the parliament is statistically representative of voters, and more important that it acts properly in the interests of the citizens, i.e. composition is less important than decisions.

In his excellent summary of these two positions, Iain McLean (1991: 172) observes that each 'seems entirely reasonable, but they are inconsistent'. There is no reconciliation: either you support one perspective or you support the other. Either you are in favour of a parliament which is a microcosm of society or, instead, you have a view of parliament which stresses its ability to act properly in the interests of all citizens. Ultimately it is a normative judgment call: 'The PR school looks at the composition of a parliament; major-itarians look at its decisions' (McLean, 1991: 175). On this basis, therefore, we can see that it is not possible to draw firm conclusions as to which is better, a proportional or a non-proportional electoral system. There are, however, other more empirical areas where conclusions can be drawn. Some systems are apparently associated with greater degrees of governmental stability while other systems promote smaller parties better than others. There are effects on the nature of parliamentary representation (e.g. 'delegate' vs. 'trustee' roles), and on the organization and campaign styles of political parties. It is possible to be far more definitive in assessing these themes, and we will return to them in chapter 7.

1.4 Built-in distortions to electoral systems

As will become all too readily apparent in due course, no single electoral system achieves full proportionality: all electoral systems distort the election result, with some parties benefiting more than others. The best a proportional electoral system can hope to achieve is to minimize the degree of distortion.

Quite apart from the 'natural' distorting effects of electoral systems (which are the subject of chapter 7), there are instances where electoral engineers resort to added 'artificial' measures, seeking to direct the distorting effects in their favour. There are four such measures which merit discussion here: two which are most common to non-proportional systems, characterized as they are by constituency representation, and two which are generally found in proportional systems where efforts are made to minimize the explosion of minor (and especially extremist) parties. Let us deal with each in turn.

First, there is the practice of *malapportionment*. This refers to a situation in which there are imbalances in the population densities of constituencies which favour some parties over others. This can happen as a matter of course, by population shifts not being compensated for by a redrawing of constituency boundaries, but it can also be engineered on purpose. Take, for example, the case of a governing party reliant on rural votes which fails to redraw the constituency boundaries to take account of rural depopulation. Malapportionment was a serious problem in the USA prior to the 1960s when the Supreme Court started to play a more active role in ordering the regular reapportionment of district boundaries.

It is possible to build in measures in the country's electoral laws to protect against such practices. The current Irish constitution, for example, which was ratified in 1937, contains a clause which ensures that each MP must represent between 20,000–30,000 voters. If the government does not meet this requirement it faces a constitutional challenge. In 1968 the governing Fianna Fáil party (whose traditional electoral base is rural) sought to have this clause diluted in a constitutional referendum, but was resoundly defeated.

A second strategy commonly employed in non-proportional electoral systems is *gerrymandering*. This refers to the practice in which constituency boundaries are redrawn with the intention of producing an inflated number of seats for a party, usually the governing party. There are two ways of achieving this. The first method is to divide one party's supporters into smaller pockets across a range of constituencies to ensure that they are kept in a permanent minority in each of the constituencies formed, thereby preventing this party from winning any seats. Wherever the party is too large to allow such a method to work, an alternative tack is to try to minimize the number of seats it can win by designing the constituency boundaries in such a way that where the governing party's vote is high it stands to win a lot of seats and where it is low it stands to lose a few seats.

The term 'gerrymander' came from the shape of a constituency designed by Governor Elbridge Gerry of Massachusetts in 1812. It was so long, narrow and wiggly that one journalist thought it looked like a salamander, and it was accordingly dubbed a 'gerrymander'. Gerrymandering is a common phenomenon in the USA where the parties have perfected systems of 'redistricting' to their advantage in those areas where they are in power. For instance, Douglas Amy (1993: 44) refers to a case in the 1990 House of Representatives election in Texas where the Democrats won ten of the fourteen congressional seats despite the fact that the Republicans had virtually the same vote: the vote tally was Democrats, 1,083,351, Republicans, 1,080,788. Amy argues that, at least in part, this reflected a successful gerrymander. A more famous example was in California in 1982 where one constituency (or district) 'designed to protect the incumbent Democrat . . . was an incredible 385-sided figure' (Amy, 1993: 46).

Gerrymandering is common to all non-proportional electoral systems, the UK included (Johnston, 1986). For instance, a frequent criticism of the Stormont government in Northern Ireland (in existence from 1920–72) was that it practised a comprehensive system of gerrymandering to protect the interests of the majority Protestant population (for a review, see Whyte, 1983).

Gerrymandering is generally associated with non-proportional electoral systems which have single-member constituencies. However, there are instances of its use in proportional systems, particularly in the case of the STV electoral system which is characterized by multi-member constituencies (Mair, 1986). The most notorious example in recent Irish history was in the mid-1970s when the minister responsible for boundary revision, James Tully, sought to redesign the constituency boundaries to benefit the governing coalition of Fine Gael and Labour. In the subsequent 1977 election the plan backfired badly largely due to the fact that the swing against the governing parties was much higher than anticipated. As a result, the loss for the governing parties was exaggerated by the effects of the attempted gerrymander. As Richard Sinnott (1993: 79) has noted, this 'incident has contributed a new term to the political lexicon. The minister responsible was James Tully, and a tullymander is a gerrymander that has an effect opposite to that intended'.

For established, mainstream politicians, one of the drawbacks of proportional systems is that they tend to produce proportional results! It is easier for smaller parties and for independents to win seats. There is a danger that counted among these will be political extremists, who in the eyes of the established politicians threaten democracy and give proportional representation (PR) a bad name. To try to minimize the risk of too many minor (and especially extremist) parties it is common for PR systems to include *minimum electoral thresholds* (usually a minimum vote percentage or a minimum number of seats won) which a party must pass in order to be granted any seats in the parliament. Therefore, even if under the electoral rules a party could actually win some seats, if it fails to surpass the threshold it is not awarded any. The most famous of these electoral thresholds operates in Germany. After the unstable experiences of PR under the Weimar Republic (1919–33) where successive governments were held hostage to the vagaries of minor parties, the German system operates a rule that a party must win either 5 per cent of the vote or three constituency seats in order to pass the electoral threshold (for further discussion, see chapter 5).

As we shall see in chapter 4, electoral thresholds are quite a common feature of PR systems. For instance, in Denmark a party needs at least 2 per cent of the national vote to gain parliamentary representation. In Sweden a party must either win 4 per cent of the national vote or else 12 per cent of the vote in one constituency to be eligible for seats. However, not all electoral thresholds are quite so onerous. In the Netherlands a party needs just 0.67 per cent of the vote to qualify for seats, and in other systems a party which fails to pass a minimum electoral threshold is allowed to keep the seats it wins, but is prevented from receiving what are known as 'top-up' seats, thereby ensuring an in-built advantage to the larger parties. Such top-up advantages are enjoyed by larger parties in Austria, Greece, Iceland, Norway and for a time in Malta (for more details and discussion, see chapter 4).

A final means of distorting the translation of votes to seats is to introduce a range of *party laws* to restrict the activities of certain categories of parties. The most controversial of these laws are ones which seek to ban parties from running in elections or, at least, to make it difficult for them. Again Germany offers the best example with its party law banning 'anti-system' parties (Poguntke, 1994). Less explicit are the various legal restrictions on the operation of certain types of party. For instance, in the 1980s in Northern Ireland a full panoply of legal restrictions were brought into play which made life very difficult for the Sinn Féin party. Its candidates were banned from the airwaves (until 1995), except during the final three weeks or so of the formal election campaign. (A similar ban in the Irish Republic from 1973–95 was even more restrictive in that it included the election campaign.) Also a matter of some controversy for Sinn Féin candidates was the non-violence declaration which all Northern Ireland candidates were required to sign.

1.5 Conclusion

In general, however, there is relatively little the established politicians can do to try to influence the effects of electoral systems on the political process. Ultimately the main factor determining the influence an electoral system can bring to bear on a polity is the way in which it has been designed, whether in terms of the degree of electoral proportionality it produces, the type of party system it engenders, the degree of choice it offers to the voter or other such factors. These issues can only be assessed through an examination of the different electoral systems on offer, exploring how they operate and with what consequences. This is the function of the remainder of this book which examines each of the five main electoral systems in operation starting, in chapter 2, with the oldest and simplest – FPTP. The book concludes, in chapter 7, with an overall assessment of the political consequences of electoral systems.

2

THE FIRST PAST THE POST ELECTORAL SYSTEM

Depending on which author one reads the first past the post (FPTP) electoral system is known by a number of titles such as 'plurality', 'relative majority', 'simple majority' or 'single member simple plurality'. Technically speaking, the most accurate title is plurality; here we will follow the more common practice of referring to it as FPTP. Under this system all a candidate needs to win a seat is more votes than any of the other candidates, but not necessarily an overall majority of all the votes cast in the constituency. It is used for elections in Britain (and for Westminster elections in Northern Ireland), the USA, Canada, India, Bangladesh, Philippines, Zambia, Nepal, Thailand and Chile. Historically the trend has been away from FPTP and towards proportional systems (as will be evident in later chapters). Most recently, FPTP has been replaced by the two-vote system in New Zealand, and by list proportional representation (PR) in South Africa. In this context, it is also worth noting that none of the newly emerging democracies, in Mediterranean Europe (i.e. in Greece, Portugal and Spain) in the 1970s or in eastern and central Europe and the former Soviet Union in the 1980s, adopted FPTP as the new electoral system. Without exception they have all opted for list systems or the two-vote variant (more on this in later chapters). This chapter focuses primarily on the operation of FPTP and the debate on its possible reform in the British context. In section 2.5 some attention is paid to the debates in other FPTP countries.

In the discussions about the British electoral system and its possible reform, three main themes resonate: simplicity, stability and constituency representation. First, the system is easy to understand: it is simple and straightforward. In the polling booth, all the voter has to do is mark an 'X' next to his or her preferred candidate. The result is also simple to understand: whoever gets the most votes – i.e. whoever gets a plurality of the votes or is, as they say, 'first past the post' – wins. This point about simplicity is particularly apt when, as we see later, comparisons are drawn with the ordinal ballots used in STV elections, or the 'Droop quota', or the concepts of largest remainders or highest averages.

Second, the argument is usually made that FPTP produces stable government and, by extension, a stable political system. British governments generally enjoy large parliamentary majorities. Indeed, for some time, this distortive tendency in FPTP was said to have law-like status, referred to as the 'cube law' on how votes are translated into seats. Coalition government is virtually unknown, unlike the rest of western Europe where the norm is coalition governments. The government, so the argument goes, is not hostage to the vagaries of relying on small (often extremist) parties for legislative support. The voters know that the party with the most seats forms the next government, unlike the situation common in the rest of western Europe where governments are formed as a result of agreements struck between party leaders in smoke-filled rooms after the election. The 'result', i.e. the determination of who forms the government, is both more democratic and fair.

Third, a central feature of British political life is constituency representation. (Note that here 'representation' is taken in its 'principal-agent' conception rather than the 'microcosmic' conception.) Each member of parliament represents a constituency. Each voter has a constituency MP who can be approached. This is in stark contrast to the situation in, say, Israel where the entire country is one vast constituency, where there may be a concentration of MPs from certain parts of the country, and where certain areas (especially rural, underpopulated areas) are essentially 'unrepresented' (in the sense that there is no single recognizable MP serving the area).

These themes of simplicity, stability and constituency representation will emerge repeatedly throughout this chapter. We start, in section 2.1, with a description of how FPTP works and of the kind of results it produces in British elections. Section 2.2 gives a brief history of the debate on electoral reform in Britain over the past century. Section 2.3 deals with the contemporary debate and assesses the prospects for change, while section 2.4 analyses the views of British voters on the issue of electoral reform. Section 2.5 briefly reviews the debates on electoral reform in three other FPTP countries, the USA, Canada and New Zealand.

2.1 The British electoral system in practice

FPTP is such an easy system to understand that it requires little explanation – and certainly nothing like the detailed explanations required for the other systems in later chapters. To aid comparison with the other systems dealt with in this book, FPTP's main points will be described according to three main features of electoral systems: *district magnitude*, *ballot structure* and *electoral formula*. These terms may sound grandiose and confusing, but in fact they refer to very simple concepts.

First, under FPTP, the UK is divided into a number of constituencies (651 in 1992; this is set to rise to 659 after boundary revisions), each electing one MP. In terms of the electoral systems' literature this is referred to as a *district magnitude* of one. This is *the* central feature distinguishing proportional and non-proportional systems. Single-seat constituencies do not produce proportional results because large numbers of voters do not support the winning candidate. Proportional results require multi-seat constituencies. Basically – as we see in later chapters – the larger the district magnitude (i.e. the more seats, or MPs, per constituency), the more proportional the result. (It is important to note that this rule only applies in PR systems. In FPTP and majoritarian electoral systems the relationship is actually reversed: the more seats per constituency the less proportional the result.)

Second, the election contest in each constituency is between candidates, not (as happens in list systems) between parties. The voting act consists of a voter placing an 'X' next to the name of his or her preferred candidate (usually representing his or her preferred party). The voter can place only one 'X', declaring a preference for just one candidate. In Figure 2.1 we see an example of a British ballot paper. The act of voting is short and sweet. The voter marks 'X' next to the appropriate candidate and then drops the ballot paper into the ballot box. The whole exercise requires barely a minute to complete.

VOTE FOR ONE CANDIDATE ONLY

1	**GRIFFIN** Theresa Griffin of 16 Dovedale Road, Liverpool L18 1DW Labour Party	
2	**MORRIS** Richard James Morris of 46 Croxteth Road, Liverpool L8 3SQ Liverpool Green Party	
3.	**MUIES** Gabriel Muies of 26 Loudon Grove, Liverpool L8 8AT Independent	
4	**PRIDDIE** Hulbert Llewelyn Priddie of 10 Lesseps Road, Liverpool L8 0RD Liberal Democrat	
5	**ZSIGMOND** Carol Ann Zsigmond of 43 Rodney Street, Liverpool L1 9EW Conservative Party Candidate	

Figure 2.1   **A British first past the post ballot paper**

In the jargon of the electoral systems literature the fact that the voter has only one choice means that the FPTP *ballot structure* is 'categorical' (an either/or choice), not 'ordinal' (where a preference can be declared for more than one candidate on the ballot paper).

Third, the successful candidate is the one who receives most votes. Note that the candidate does not have to win an overall majority of votes, he or she must only have more votes than anybody else, or a plurality of support. Therefore the *electoral formula* is a plurality election. It is for this reason that FPTP is often referred to as a plurality system. The 1992 election provides an interesting example of the difference between 'plurality' and 'majority'. As Table 2.1 shows, in the constituency of Inverness, Nairn and Lochaber, Sir

Table 2.1   **An FPTP election result: Inverness, Nairn and Lochaber in 1992**

	Number of votes	Per cent of vote
Johnston, Sir Russell (Liberal Democrat)	13,258	26.0
Stewart, D. (Labour)	12,800	25.1
Ewing, F. S. (SNP)	12,562	24.7
Scott, J. (Conservative)	11,517	22.6
Martin, J. (Green)	766	1.5
Total Vote	50,903	
Turnout		73.3%

Source: Wood and Wood (1992: 143).

Russell Johnston was elected despite having only 26 per cent of the total vote in the constituency (when we allow for those who did not vote, this represents just 19 per cent of the electorate). He had a plurality of support, but not by any means an overall majority. In fact, he had just 458 votes (0.9 per cent) more than his nearest rival. To look at this from another angle, 74 per cent of those who voted in Inverness, Nairn and Lochaber did not vote for the 'winning' candidate; 81 per cent of the electorate (i.e. including those who did not vote) did not show support for him. In the 1992 British general election as a whole, 40 per cent of MPs were elected without having an overall majority of the votes in their constituency. Such an outcome is quite normal under FPTP, as evidenced by the trends over time shown in Table 2.2. Here we see that the most striking results were in the two 1974 elections when almost two-thirds of MPs were elected with less than half the total vote in their constituencies.

When the figures are aggregated across the country as a whole, it is possible to see the levels of distortion which can be produced under FPTP. Table 2.3 gives the percentage votes and seats for the three main parties in post-war British elections. The trend to follow is the percentage difference between the share of votes received and the share of seats won by each of the parties. A plus sign implies the party gained a greater share of seats than its share of the vote; a minus sign implies it received a lesser share of seats.

Clearly the most striking trend is that for the Liberals/Liberal Democrats. This party has consistently won fewer seats relative to its total vote. The starkest example was in the supposedly 'mould-breaking' election of 1983, when despite having almost as many

Table 2.2   British MPs elected with less than 50 per cent of the vote, 1918–92

	MPs elected with a minority of votes	Minority MPs as % of all MPs
1918	97	14.5
1922	173	30.0
1923	203	35.2
1924	124	21.5
1929	310	53.8
1931	34	5.9
1935	58	10.1
1945	174	29.0
1950	187	29.9
1951	39	6.2
1955	37	5.9
1959	80	12.7
1964	232	36.8
1966	185	29.4
1970	124	19.7
February 1974	408	64.3
October 1974	380	59.8
1979	207	32.6
1983	334	51.4
1987	283	43.5
1992	258	39.6

Sources: Punnett (1991); Wood and Wood (1992).

votes as Labour (25.4 per cent compared with 27.6 per cent), the Liberal/Social Democrat Alliance won a far smaller share of seats (3.5 per cent compared with 32.2 per cent): a vote–seat difference of 21.9 per cent. To show this discrepancy in another way, in 1983 on average each Conservative MP represented 32,777 voters; each Labour MP represented 40,464 voters; while each Alliance MP represented a grand total of 338,302 voters.

The large discrepancy in Liberal Democrat seats and votes is caused by the fact that the party's support is spread thinly across the country; it does not have the same levels of concentrated support in particular parts of the country which the two larger parties enjoy. The Conservative Party's electoral base is in the South of England; Labour's electoral base is in the North, and in Scotland and Wales. Similarly the small regional parties in Scotland, Wales and Northern Ireland benefit from a strong local focus in support and, on the whole, they tend to win an appropriate share of seats relative to their share of the vote. In a recent detailed analysis of geographical trends in voting behaviour, Pattie *et al.* (1992: 142) conclude that the regional divide 'has been a feature of British politics since the 1974 elections, and has widened appreciably during the 1980s' (though, in 1992, they find evidence to suggest that the growth in the regional divide was halted (Pattie *et al.*, 1993)). This conclusion is supported by an analysis of regional trends in electoral disproportionality by Patrick Dunleavy and his colleagues (1993). They find that, in the 1955–92 period, the Conservative Party benefited greatly by winning more seats than its vote warranted in the South-East, the South-West and East Anglia. Labour benefited – though less markedly – in the North, Scotland and Wales.

The other point to note about the trend in vote–seat per cent differences in Table 2.3 is that the differences have become larger in recent elections. This reflects the fact that the Liberal surge in votes

Table 2.3   **British election results, 1945–92: vote and seat percentages.**

	Conservatives			Labour			Liberals/Liberal Democrats[a]		
	Vote (%)	Seat (%)	Diff. (%)	Vote (%)	Seat (%)	Diff. (%)	Vote (%)	Seat (%)	Diff. (%)
1945	36.8	31.1	−5.7	48.0	61.4	+13.4	9.0	1.9	−7.1
1950	43.4	47.7	+4.3	46.1	50.4	+4.3	9.1	1.4	−7.7
1951	48.0	51.4	+3.4	48.8	47.2	−1.6	2.6	1.0	−1.6
1955	49.7	54.8	+5.1	46.4	44.0	−2.4	2.7	1.0	−1.7
1959	49.4	57.9	+8.5	43.8	41.0	−2.8	5.9	1.0	−4.9
1964	43.4	48.3	+4.9	44.1	50.3	+6.2	11.2	1.4	−9.8
1966	41.9	40.2	−1.7	48.0	57.8	+9.8	8.5	1.9	−6.6
1970	46.4	52.4	+6.0	43.1	45.7	+2.6	7.5	1.0	−6.5
Feb. 1974	37.9	46.8	+8.9	37.2	47.4	+10.2	19.3	2.2	−17.1
Oct. 1974	35.8	43.6	+7.8	39.3	50.2	+10.9	18.3	2.0	−16.3
1979	43.9	53.4	+9.5	36.9	42.4	+5.5	13.8	1.7	−12.1
1983	42.4	61.1	+18.7	27.6	32.2	+4.6	25.4	3.5	−21.9
1987	42.3	57.8	+15.5	30.8	35.2	+4.4	22.6	3.4	−19.2
1992	41.9	51.6	+9.7	34.4	41.6	+7.2	17.8	3.1	−14.7

Notes: Percentages do not add up to 100 because not all parties are included. In the 'diff.' columns a positive sign implies that the party gained a greater share of seats than its share of the vote, a negative sign implies it received a lesser share of seats.
[a] Includes the Social Democratic Party in 1983 and 1987.
Sources: Mackie and Rose (1991); 1992 election results.

has coincided with a decline in the total vote for the two larger parties. This trend is clearly shown in Figure 2.2 which traces the decline in the Conservative and Labour vote and the rise in the level of vote–seat per cent differences for the Liberals/Liberal Democrats. What this demonstrates is that FPTP works best in a two-party system. In a multi-party system – as the 1983 results indicate – there are bound to be some gross anomalies (see also Dunleavy, 1991; Dunleavy *et al.*, 1993; Dunleavy and Margetts, 1995; Norris, 1995).

A third point to be noted about the figures in Table 2.3 is that the system can also produce unusual election results in terms of who 'wins' office. In 1951 the Conservative Party won more seats than Labour despite having fewer votes. In February 1974 it was Labour's turn to benefit, winning more seats than the Conservatives despite having fewer votes. As for the point about strong government, the only example of a 'hung' parliament (where no single party had an overall majority) was in February 1974. We have to go back to before the Second World War to find other examples (1929, 1923, twice in 1910). However, there have been a number of governments with very small majorities, where the practice of 'strong' government has been somewhat curtailed. The most prominent example was as a result of the October 1974 election when Labour had only a majority of three.

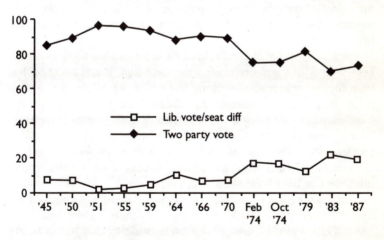

Figure 2.2   British two-party support and levels of vote–seat differences for the 'third' party.

By April 1976, due to resignations and by-election losses, the government had lost majority status and for the remainder of its term it relied on the support of smaller parties, especially the Liberals. (This was the period of the 'Lib–Lab pact'.) Among the other close election results are those in 1950 (when Labour had a majority of five seats) and 1964 (when Labour's majority was four). The current Conservative government was elected in 1992 with a majority of just twenty-one seats, leaving the government vulnerable to backbench revolts. Due to a process of attrition (primarily death and subsequent loss of by-elections, and in some cases desertion to other parties) the government's majority was gradually whittled away. By early 1996 it was close to losing its majority.

2.2 Debates about electoral reform in the UK

The question of electoral reform has gained a certain prominence in recent years, though not for the first time. As an examination of late nineteenth- and early twentieth-century British history shows, the electoral system was a major issue in parliamentary debates relating to the development of democracy (Bogdanor, 1981; Butler, 1963; Hart, 1992). Indeed, on one occasion – in 1918 – the single transferable vote (STV) was very nearly adopted as the method of election for a third of constituencies. Furthermore it is interesting to note how the main themes of the debate have not changed a great deal over time.

Because the issue of electoral reform in Britain has been so closely bound up with the process of democratization, much attention has been focused on areas of electoral law which are unrelated to voting rules. In particular, attention has focused on the process of enfranchisement – on the gradual extension of voting rights to men and later to women – and on constituency boundaries and their revision (Butler, 1963). These issues are not dealt with in this section; here we are more concerned with the electoral system itself, i.e. the voting rules used in British elections.

The main period of debate was from the mid-nineteenth century through to the early 1930s. A series of attempts – most notably in 1884, 1910, 1916–17, and 1931 – were made to change the voting rules for election to the House of Commons. This coincided with the development of democracy, mass enfranchisement and the origins of the existing party system. Three electoral systems featured in these debates: the limited vote, the alternative vote and the STV. It was the latter of these which attracted the most attention, particularly among those pushing for change. STV originated in the writings of Thomas Hare from the 1850s onwards. His work – particularly his *Treatise on the Election of Representatives, Parliamentary and Municipal* (1859) – greatly affected people like the philosopher, John Stuart Mill, who at the time was a member of parliament (Hart, 1992). Mill sought unsuccessfully to have Hare's STV system ('hare-brained' as it was dubbed by critics) introduced in the 1860s. Later, in the 1880s, the PR Society was formed with the principal aim of lobbying for STV.

Looked at from today's perspective, there is something quite familiar about a number of aspects of these early debates. First, there is a close similarity in the nature of the people calling for electoral reform. In the 1880s and early 1900s the PR Society featured prominently, working in coalition with minority groupings in the major parties. Similar coalitions between groups within the main parties and the Electoral Reform Society (the successor to the PR Society) are prominent in the current debate. Second – and seemingly in stark contrast to the 'founding fathers' of the USA (McLean, 1992) – there is not a lot of evidence that British politicians took much trouble to study electoral systems and to understand them. Jennifer Hart's (1992) study of the earlier debates shows how little critics of electoral reform seemed to know about the workings of electoral systems. Similar observations are not uncommon in the contemporary debate.

Finally, there are evident similarities in the themes which featured in both debates. In both cases the principal theme has been strong government. However, in the earlier debates whereas there was a concern to protect minority interests, this was not in the sense we would understand today, where PR is often proposed to facilitate the representation of ethnic minorities, but rather in the sense that the position of the minority elite was seen as endangered by the process of mass enfranchisement. The elite faced the prospect of losing power to the masses, and in this sense 'strong government' was under threat. There was also a desire to limit the power of parties, to control the dangers to democracy of factions and caucuses (particularly as, it was felt, these have a tendency to encourage extremes).

These questions were behind one significant change in the electoral system (in 1867) and several more ambitious proposals for change which were all defeated in the Commons. The change was the adoption of what was called the limited vote for thirteen three-seat constituencies and one four-seat constituency introduced by the Reform Act of that year.[1] Prior to the Reform Act, most of the parliamentary constituencies elected two members, which tended to exaggerate the bias in favour of larger parties inherent in FPTP. Under the limited vote system, electors were given three votes in a four-seat constituency and two votes in a three-seat constituency. As Bogdanor (1981: 101) observes, its intention was to 'allow [a] minority to be represented on as little as one-third of the vote'. While there is some evidence that the system did help to protect minority interests, it did not do so consistently (Lakeman, 1970: 81–2). Furthermore, it 'encouraged the development of a party machine whose purpose it was to ensure that only majorities were represented' via elaborate vote management strategies (Bogdanor, 1981: 104).

The Third Reform Act of 1884–5 abolished the limited vote and with it went most of Britain's multi-seat constituencies. The single-seat constituencies date from this period. One main consequence of the experiment with the limited vote was that it weakened the case for further attempts at electoral reform. There was little appetite for another experiment. This reluctance was clear in each of the subsequent pushes for electoral reform in 1884, 1910, 1916–17 and 1931. Each of these episodes is dealt with in detail in the available histories (Bogdanor, 1981; Butler, 1964; Hart, 1992). It is worthwhile spending a moment on the 1916–17 Speaker's Conference proposals as this was the one occasion when the electoral reformers came enticingly close to getting their way. In 1916 a Speaker's Conference was established to come up with proposals relating to franchise extension and its consequences. Its 1917 report proposed STV for borough constituencies – about a third of the constituencies – and the alternative vote (used in Australia, and discussed in chapter 3) for the remaining (predominantly rural) constituencies. It was the STV proposal which attracted the bulk of attention. Here was a clear attempt to protect the minority elite from the dangers of mass enfranchisement, particularly in urban areas where the Labour Party stood to make great gains. The proposal attracted widespread support in the subsequent parliamentary debate, particularly among those members not affected by it. Ultimately, it was rejected, but only after a series of votes in the Commons and in the Lords in which the proposal was repeatedly rejected and re-introduced. Indeed, its initial rejection, in the first Commons vote, was by only a narrow margin. Just eight votes prevented the adoption of STV for one-third of constituencies. The result could not have been closer. With the rejection of the proposal, and 'as a rather picturesque anomaly' (Bogdanor, 1981: 129), STV was introduced in only four of the seven university seats (representing university graduates; see Blackburn, 1995: 70–1). Otherwise the electoral system remained unchanged.

With the exception of one more push for electoral reform in 1931 – when the alternative vote was the system being promoted – nothing much was heard on the question until the early 1970s. Then a number of factors coincided to drive electoral reform back onto the agenda. The most significant of these was the growing instability of the British voter as revealed by the 1974 election results (see Denver, 1994; Farrell *et al.*, 1994). As was discussed above when examining Table 2.3, the evidently unfair result for the Liberal Party in that year, whose large votes in both elections were not translated into large numbers of seats, and the disproportionate benefit in seats for Labour in February 1974 (when the party received more seats than the Conservatives despite having fewer votes), once again raised questions about the electoral system. By the mid-1970s, the advocates of electoral reform were no longer being dismissed as 'harmless and rather amusing cranks, like nudists or the eaters of nut-cutlets' (Lord Avebury cited in Hart, 1992: 279). Indeed, they received a further fillip from three more developments in the 1970s: the collapse of the Stormont political system in Northern Ireland, Britain's accession to the European Community, and the devolution debate.

It was the outbreak of the 'troubles' in Northern Ireland which was to see the first real move towards PR in the UK. As part of its effort to reduce communal tensions in Northern Ireland (which was now under direct rule from London for the first time since 1920), the British government re-introduced the single transferable vote in the province for all elections other than Westminster elections. In the original Government of Ireland Act of 1920 STV had been proposed for the newly created Northern Ireland state, but in the 1920s the Stormont government replaced it by FPTP. At least partially in consequence, the electoral history of Northern Ireland from the 1920s to the 1960s was one of consistent electoral dominance by the Unionist majority, in large part facilitated by the electoral system. In 1973 STV was re-introduced for local elections and for elections to the new Assembly established as a result of Anglo-Irish talks at

Sunningdale. Subsequently in 1979 STV was further extended to European Parliament elections in Northern Ireland.

The second push for PR came with the accession of Britain (together with Denmark and Ireland) to the European Community, which coincided with discussions about the introduction of uniform electoral procedures in the first direct elections to the European Parliament. To date, the issue of uniform electoral procedures has yet to be resolved and as a result there are a range of different electoral systems being applied in the fifteen member states (Bowler and Farrell, 1993). For a while, in the mid-1970s, it looked as if the matter would be resolved in favour of some form of PR and therefore the issue attracted much attention in the House of Commons. In 1976 a free vote was held on Britain's system for European Parliament elections, in which MPs were asked to decide between adopting a regional list system (referred to in the debates as the 'Finnish system') or FPTP (Bogdanor, 1981: 163–8). The list system was proposed because STV was too closely associated with the Liberal Party and therefore it was believed that Labour MPs would not support it. In the event, Labour MPs divided roughly in half and the Conservatives under their new leader, Margaret Thatcher (who was stridently against PR), voted overwhelmingly against. The motion was lost and FPTP became the chosen system.

The third and most significant push for PR was associated with the debates over Scottish and Welsh devolution. The 1973 report of the Kilbrandon Commission on the Constitution had recommended STV, together with the alternative vote for sparsely populated parts of Scotland, but these proposals were not incorporated in the subsequent 1977 devolution bill. The regional parties and the Liberals favoured STV; the Labour government – understandably, given that both Scotland and Wales are Labour strongholds – did not. This lack of consensus between the two sides ensured the failure of the devolution bill.

The coincidence of electoral instability, and the regional and EC debates, meant that electoral reform was high on the political agenda. In 1976 the Hansard Society established a Commission on Electoral Reform, chaired by the historian and Conservative peer, Lord Blake. Its report in the same year proposed a version of the additional member system (i.e. the system used in Germany, referred to in chapter 5 as the 'two-vote' system), with three-quarters of the Commons elected in single-seat constituencies and the remainder elected on regional lists (for an assessment of this proposal, see chapter 5 below). The fact that this Commission was self-appointed, that its membership was not seen as representative of the different political groupings and that it was financed by industry, affected the reception of its report, but it managed to attract considerable attention none the less. Coinciding with the report, an all-party National Committee for Electoral Reform was established, chaired by Lord Harlech. This was designed to coordinate the various organizations calling for reform, and it too attracted a great deal of attention. After several years of appearing neutral as to which PR system to promote, it eventually came down firmly in favour of STV.

Largely as a result of the activities of the National Committee and its influential backers, electoral reform remained on the agenda of British politics into the 1980s. However, the fact remained that, for the most part, electoral reform was the concern of smaller parties and small minorities within the larger parties. Neither the Conservative nor Labour hierarchies were prepared to embrace electoral reform, fearing that this would endanger their chances of forming single-party majority governments. By the end of the 1980s, however – and after having lost three elections in succession – the Labour Party began to show signs of a new emphasis. The view was being expressed more frequently within party ranks that it could no longer hope to defeat the Conservatives by itself, that some form of coalition was inevitable. Given the long-held view of the Liberals (now Liberal Democrats) in favour of PR, this meant that any future coalition arrangement with them would be likely to have to include an agreement on electoral reform. In 1990 the Labour Party established a working party on electoral reform, chaired by the academic, Raymond Plant (who was subsequently elevated to a peerage). This met over a period of two years, during which time it produced two interim reports. Its final report, published in 1993, proposed a majoritarian electoral system for elections to the House of Commons (Labour Party, 1993). As we shall see in chapter 3, this 'supplementary vote' system is very similar to the alternative vote system used in Australia. In the subsequent party conference, in a move led by the Labour leader, John Smith, the party voted in favour of a referendum on election reform, effectively shelving that part of the Plant Report which related to national level elections and once again raising the possibility of a shift towards a PR system (Norris, 1995).

The British electoral system remains on the agenda, especially after Labour's fourth successive electoral defeat in 1992. Obviously it is impossible to tell, at this stage, where it will all lead, but there is little evidence that the issue of electoral reform will simply 'go away'. It is, therefore, useful to examine the main arguments that are generally made by the protagonists.

2.3 Does Britain need a new electoral system?

To provide an informed answer to this question we first have to consider the alternatives, which is the function of the rest of this book. In chapter 7, having examined the main electoral systems in use in other countries, we will return to this question. There is, however, another perspective to consider based on what we know of the British electoral system and British politics, and that is the extent to which FPTP performs to expectations. In particular, to what extent does it meet the requirements of simplicity, stability and constituency representation which were introduced at the start of the chapter? Indeed, to what extent are these requirements all relevant?

It cannot be disputed that FPTP is simple, both to use and to understand, and this fact will be ever more evident as we examine the other main systems in use, but is simplicity really the issue? It is all very well being able to understand what is going on, but what is actually gained if a voter's preferred candidate (and preferred party) is resoundingly defeated election after election, perhaps, because the voter happens to live in a non-marginal constituency? In other words, the benefit of simplicity can be (and is often) at the cost of fairness to smaller parties, to the supporters of smaller parties and to those voters 'trapped' in seats which are safely held by parties they do not support.

Why should the question of simplicity be any more important for British voters than for any other voters? It clearly has not been seen as a relevant factor by those countries which have recently adopted PR systems: in Mediterranean, central and eastern Europe; Japan, or New Zealand – the latter replacing FPTP by a variant of the two-vote (or additional member) system. Indeed, it is hard to find any evidence of higher levels of voter confusion in other countries. For instance, there are no perceptible differences in the numbers of spoiled or invalid votes. For that matter, when Northern Ireland voters moved towards STV for local elections in the 1970s, 'the system [did not] prove complicated for voters': the numbers of invalid votes did not rise (Bogdanor, 1981: 147).

There are a number of issues to consider under the rubric of government 'stability', and we will be returning to this, in far more detail, in chapter 7. For the moment, let us deal with one aspect which is prominent in the British debate, namely the argument that FPTP has a built-in mechanism to produce single-party parliamentary majorities and hence 'strong' government. Over the years this has been formalized as a 'cube rule' of FPTP systems (Butler, 1963; Kendall and Stuart, 1950), which can be summarized as follows: if the ratio of votes that two parties receive is A : B, then this will result in the following ratio of seats, $A^3 : B^3$. In other words, FPTP is said to exaggerate the winning party's lead, making it easier to win a clear majority of the seats, and hence promoting greater parliamentary stability. Writing in the 1960s, the leading British psephologist, David Butler (1963: 194) concluded: 'The British electoral system is not a gamble . . . The theoretical possibility of quite haphazard results arising from any given division of votes is undeniable; the practical improbability is so great under present conditions that it need not be considered.'

The cube rule has attracted great interest in the academic literature, and in recent years it has been argued that the post-war British record suggests that rather than the power index being three, it would be more accurate to set it at 2.5 (Laakso, 1979) or 2.6 (Taagepera and Shugart, 1989). More critically, however, is the point that, since Butler, British electoral results have become far less predictable. Voter volatility and the electoral rise of the Liberals/Liberal Democrats have made it more difficult to predict the relationship between votes and seats, leading Vernon Bogdanor (1981: 180; also Butler, 1983; Curtice and Steed, 1982; for an alternative perspective, see Norris and Crewe, 1994) to conclude that 'the cube law has ceased to hold in Britain'. This is confirmed by analysis of the 1992 election result which shows no perceptible evidence of vote–seat distortion (Curtice, 1992). If the system can no longer guarantee a parliamentary majority for the party winning the most votes (as evidenced by the 1974 results), then this raises doubts about the utility of the argument that FPTP promotes stable government.

Despite the evident demise of the 'cube rule', it can be argued that the record of post-war British electoral politics speaks for itself.

British governments have tended to be long-lasting and stable, in contrast to the record of other European countries. Here attention is paid to the instability of coalitions, and the dangers that can hold for political system stability. The common examples cited are Fourth Republic France (1946–58), Weimar Germany (1919–33) and contemporary Italy. More recently, there have been references to the frequency of elections in Ireland since the early 1980s, especially the three elections held over an eighteen-month period in 1981–2. Here 'stability' is taken to mean 'longevity': that is, the length of time governments remain in office. While it is easy to refer to unstable cases like Italy – which has tended to change government virtually every year – it is also quite easy to find examples of countries, like Luxembourg or Sweden, where coalition governments are the norm and yet where governments enjoy long lives. We will return to this issue in chapter 7 when dealing with international comparisons and other meanings of the word 'stability'.

The third requirement of an electoral system, according to the British debate, is that it should incorporate constituency representation. Just like the legend of the 'Bobby on the beat', there tends to be a certain nostalgic imagery attached to the idea of the constituency politician – to the idea that voters throughout the land have constituency representatives promoting their special interests and needs. For instance, this was a major factor behind the decision of the Labour Party's Plant Commission to propose the 'supplementary vote' electoral system for Britain, where the country would retain the tradition of single-seat constituencies (see chapter 3 below). Equally this is why, as we saw, the debates about electoral reform over the years have always focused on the alternative vote (used in Australia), STV (used in Ireland) or the two-vote system (used in Germany) as alternatives for parliamentary elections. A central feature of all these systems, as we shall see in later chapters, is constituency representation. In other words, there are other systems available which incorporate constituency representation; FPTP is not the only system to do so.

The question remains, how significant a factor is constituency representation? For instance, to what extent can one argue that Sir Russell Johnston had a proper mandate to represent his constituency, when only 19 per cent of the electorate actually voted for him? Similar questions can be raised about those 40 per cent of MPs elected in 1992 without an overall majority of support in their constituency. Furthermore, what significance has constituency representation in a parliamentary party system which discourages independent action; where MPs are whipped into the voting lobbies? There is not exactly great scope for individual constituency representation in the legislature when MPs are expected to toe the party line. This is not to deny the fact that constituent contact with MPs is significant and increasing, that MPs are making greater use of parliamentary question time to promote constituency concerns (Cain *et al.*, 1987; Franklin and Norton, 1993), and that such activities clearly affect the personal vote of MPs (Norton and Wood, 1990). However, parliamentary questions represent only a part of the work of the Commons; it is in the area of the legislative role of MPs that questions could perhaps be raised. A politician who pays attention to constituency concerns may not have quite so much time to devote to legislative details (Bowler and Farrell, 1993).

There are other questions worth raising concerning the issue of constituency representation. For instance, there is a question mark over the representation of those voters who backed a losing candidate (e.g. to what extent are the interests of a Tory supporter being served by a sitting Labour MP?). Finally, there is the issue of whether, in fact, constituency representation is compatible with stable government. Almost by definition a good constituency MP (particularly if from the governing party) is not necessarily a good team player in parliament. In cases in which specific constituency interests conflict with party policy an MP may be unwilling or unable to toe the party line. Given the right circumstances, this could threaten government stability.

2.4 Does Britain want a new electoral system?

Whether or not we can arrive at a theoretical conclusion in favour of, or against, electoral reform, there is still the question of public opinion. Regardless of the issue of whether FPTP actually achieves its objectives of simplicity, stability and constituency representation, what levels of support are there for maintaining it as Britain's electoral system? The on-going debate on electoral reform has in recent years provoked some attention to public attitudes towards the electoral system (for a review, see Weir, 1992). As Table 2.4 indicates, the evidence is not conclusive either way. According to

Table 2.4   Levels of support for electoral reform in Britain in 1992–95

(N)	NOP/BBC 1992 (2,288) (%)	Harris/ITN 1992 (4,701) (%)	Rowntree/ ICM 1992 (9,600) (%)	Joseph Rowntree Reform Trust/ MORI 1995 (2,141) (%)
In favour of electoral reform	37	43	59	61
Against electoral reform	44	52	27	20
Neutral	19	5	15	19

Notes: The precise questions on which the figures are based are as follows: NOP/ BBC: 'Do you think we should scrap the present first past the post system for electing MPs and introduce proportional representation? Yes, introduce proportional representation; No, keep present system; Don't know.' Harris/ITN: 'Do you believe that the system of electing MPs should be changed from the present first past the post method to a form of proportional representation? Change from proportional representation; Keep the present system; Not stated.' Rowntree/ICM and Joseph Rowntree Reform Trust/MORI: 'This country should adopt a new voting system that would give parties seats in parliament in proportion to their share of the votes. Agree; Disagree; Neutral or don't know.'
Sources: Dunleavy *et al.* (1993); Kellner (1992); Joseph Rowntree Reform Trust/ MORI *State of the Nation* poll, April–May 1995.

Peter Kellner's reading (1992: 10) of the evidence (based on columns 1 and 2 of Table 2.4), 'reform is less popular with the public than its advocates supposed'. Both the NOP/BBC and the Harris/ITN exit polls of voters in the 1992 general election indicated that a plurality of voters were against changing the electoral system. This is in contrast to evidence from polls earlier in 1992 where there were far greater levels of support for electoral reform.

In part, these differences obviously reflected variations in question wording, but, according to Kellner, they also evidenced a shift in public mood. Kellner suggests that the earlier support for electoral reform was, to an extent, due to the hypothetical nature of the question, and that this changed closer to polling day as voters became aware of the real possibility of electoral reform depending on the electoral result. He continues (1992: 11): 'If people are asked about something they seldom think about, the prospect of change has a vague, grass-is-greener, appeal. But when the same issue grows in importance and change becomes a real possibility, then suddenly the status quo, with its comforting familiarity, looks less dreadful.'

According to the perspective of Dunleavy *et al.* (1993: 179), Kellner's approach to this question is inadequate, particularly as it is based on 'crude or overly complex single questions'. They argue that a better strategy for assessing public attitudes towards electoral reform is to use a number of different questions and to check for consistency in the responses. Making use of a large sample survey Dunleavy *et al.* produce findings which are strikingly different from Kellner's. The third column of Table 2.4 breaks the Dunleavy rule by presenting the responses to just one of the questions posed on electoral reform. (The final column provides the most recent (1995) data, which show little sign of change.) When account is taken of the other questions, Dunleavy *et al.* (1993: 180) find that: '43 per cent of respondents consistently backed PR while 32 per cent consistently preferred plurality rule' – a striking reversal of the proportions presented by Kellner. Furthermore, support for the current electoral system is 'concentrated increasingly among Conservative voters alone' (ibid.: 190); and there is evidence of a growing preference for electoral change among younger voters. Overall, Dunleavy *et al.* conclude that, contrary to Kellner, there is no evidence of a shift in public opinion against electoral reform; if anything the reverse seems to be happening. However they qualify this (and thereby offer some support for Kellner's position) by pointing out that support for the status quo increased when voters were reminded that it was more likely to produce single-party government. In other words, when electoral reform and its consequences were presented in a more concrete (less hypothetical) fashion, attitudes were somewhat more ambivalent.

The Dunleavy *et al.* and Kellner studies share an approach in which voters are asked, in varying degrees of abstraction, what they think about alternatives to the British electoral system. Ultimately it is difficult to tell to what extent the respondents fully understand the differences between electoral systems. Indeed, in both studies, as we have seen, there is some evidence that voters' attitudes towards electoral reform become more qualified whenever the distinctions are clarified in any way. A better way to get a true picture of voter attitudes to alternative electoral systems is to have them first use another system and then ask them what they think about it. This approach was followed in an Electoral Reform Society/MORI exit

Table 2.5 Levels of support for electoral reform in London in 1994.

(N)	All voters (3,893) (%)	18–34 years (973) (%)	55+ years (1,480) (%)	Middle class (2,196) (%)	Working class (1,353) (%)	Conservative (866) (%)	Labour (1,459) (%)	Liberal Democrat (375) (%)
In favour of PR	44	51	33	50	34	27	48	65
In favour of FPTP	45	41	54	40	54	65	43	28
Neutral	11	8	13	10	12	8	10	7

Notes: The question wording was: 'Which do you think is a fairer voting system, the one you have used on (the mock) ballot paper or the usual voting system? System just used (proportional representation); Usual system; Neither/don't know.' Where percentages do not add up to 100 this is due to rounding error. The party breakdowns are based on those respondents either very or fairly 'close' to their respective parties, i.e. ignoring those who are not very close.
Sources: MORI/Electoral Reform Society exit poll, 9 June 1994.

poll of London voters during the 1994 European Parliament elections (see Bowler and Farrell, 1994; 1996). The respondents were invited to complete a STV ballot paper which included the names of the main party candidates. They were then asked what they thought of this electoral system as opposed to the usual FPTP system. The results, in Table 2.5, offer some support for both Kellner's and Dunleavy's perspectives. On the one hand, opinion among all voters (in column 1) was equally divided between status quo (45 per cent) and change (44 per cent) – there was no tendency either way. On the other hand, when the sample is broken down it is possible to see clear pockets of support for electoral reform among younger voters (51 per cent of 18–34 year olds were in favour of electoral reform) and middle-class voters (50 per cent in favour); among Liberal Democrat supporters (65 per cent in favour); and also, to a degree, among Labour voters (48 per cent in favour). As Dunleavy *et al.* found, the most distinctive grouping of opposition to electoral reform was among Conservative voters (65 per cent against).

In general the survey evidence does not suggest a groundswell of opinion in favour of electoral reform in Britain. There are pockets of support for change – particularly among younger voters, middle-class voters and Liberal Democrat supporters – but equally (and, crucially, where it matters, among Conservative supporters) there is support for the status quo. It could be argued, however, that such agnosticism is understandable, especially given the absence of an extensive public education programme detailing the pros and cons of different electoral systems (such as occurred in New Zealand in the lead-up to its electoral reform referendums of 1992–3, see Vowles, 1995).

Thus far we have been dealing with the debate over FPTP solely in the British context. As was pointed out at the beginning of the chapter, however, there are a number of other countries which use FPTP. It is worthwhile examining the debates in some of these cases.

2.5 The electoral reform debate in other FPTP countries

Much of the literature on electoral systems focuses on the US case, however, very little of this actually deals with the voting system used in the USA. For the most part the attention is on issues of redistricting and voting rights. As Douglas Amy has recently pointed out: 'the American voting system is the aberration. Ours is one of the few developed countries that continues to cling to a plurality system, and among those few, ours is the only one in which no public debate over the desirability of this system is occurring' (Amy, 1993: 4; also Dunleavy and Margetts, 1995). It is important to stress this point. In other words, the USA represents one of the few FPTP systems in operation where there has been little sustained call for reform. As Amy's comprehensive study points out, in those instances where electoral reform is raised there is the standard battery of objections to reject it: other systems are said to be too complex, promoting the dangers of unstable government, fringe parties and the loss of constituency representation, and giving too much power to the party elites. However, the most significant reason why electoral reform does not appear on the American political agenda seems to be a basic lack of interest on the part of the voters (and presumably by implication, the elite). In other words while people may think there are problems with the system – as shown most particularly by the low levels of esteem for politicians generally and, perhaps, by very low turnout – there is no great interest in electoral reform as one possible means of changing things. Another factor which undoubtedly contributes to the lack of concern about the electoral system is the fact that the US government tends to be 'divided', in the sense that it is common for one party to control the presidency while another controls Congress. This is quite different from the British case where one party can control all of government for extended periods, due, in part, to the distorting effects of the electoral system. Finally, the nature of the US party system is an important factor in explaining the lack of concern about electoral reform in the USA. This is revealed both by the weakness of US parties (Wattenberg, 1994), which ensures little attention to national vote trends, and also by the fact that the USA 'now stands alone in the world as the homeland of a system that is almost perfectly two-party . . . [and] if only two parties run candidates then even a plurality rule system may operate quite proportionally' (Dunleavy and Margetts, 1995: 24).

Of course, the USA has not been entirely devoid of any attention to other electoral systems. Indeed in the earlier part of this century there were notable efforts to adopt STV at local government level, with some success. As Leon Weaver (1986: 140) notes: 'PR systems have been used in approximately two dozen cities (for city councils and school boards). These cases might conceivably be counted as five dozen if one wishes to count the school communities in Massachusetts PR cities and in the New York City community school boards as separate cases.' Lest we take this to mean that STV was on a dramatic growth curve in this period, it is well to note Weaver's important qualifier that 'PR systems have constituted a very small sample – a fraction of 1 per cent – when compared with the total number of electoral systems in this country' (ibid.). As we move into the second half of this century the use of STV in American local government is on a steep decline. Today it is used only in Cambridge, Massachusetts (for city council and school committee elections) and in New York City (for community school board elections). The USA also makes relatively widespread use of the second ballot system (such as used in France, see chapter 3). In some southern states (notably Louisiana) the second ballot system is even used in congressional elections.

Citizens and politicians of the USA may not be countenancing electoral system reform, but their neighbours in Canada must be giving it some thought in the light of the 1993 electoral result which saw the governing Progressive Conservative Party's number of parliamentary seats reduced from 169 (and an overall majority) to just two! As Table 2.6 shows, the Progressive Conservatives were not the only ones to receive a nasty shock from the Canadian electorate in 1993. The New Democratic Party's vote also plummeted, leaving the party with less than a quarter of the seats it had in 1988. It is no exaggeration to state that '[f]or Canada's national party system, the results of the 35th general election held on 25 October 1993 were of earthquake proportions' (Erickson, 1995: 133).

Table 2.6   **The Canadian electoral earthquake of 1993**

	Percentage of vote		Number of seats	
	1993	1988	1993	1988
Bloc Québécois	13.5	n.a.*	54	n.a.
Liberal Party	41.3	31.9	177	83
New Democratic Party	6.9	20.4	9	43
Progressive Conservative Party	16.0	43.0	2	169
Reform Party	18.7	2.1	52	0

Note: * The party was first established in 1990.
Source: Chief Electoral Officer of Canada.

Electoral reform has been mooted before in certain Canadian circles. In the 1970s, William Irvine (1979) proposed a switch towards the German two-vote system. For a long time, however, the political elite tended not to pay much attention to the issue. For instance, the Royal Commission on Electoral Reform and Party Financing, set up in 1979 to carry out a root-and-branch survey of the Canadian electoral process and how it might be reformed, was specifically excluded from examining the nature of the electoral system. In the early 1990s, this changed and as part of the negotiations over constitutional and regional reform in Canada, there was some consideration given to the issue of the electoral system and whether it should be changed, at least for elections to the upper chamber. With the failure of this constitutional talks process, electoral reform was left on the back burner. It will be of interest to see how the dramatic electoral results of 1993 might affect this debate in the longer run.

If the Canadians are looking for ideas on how to go about changing their electoral system from FPTP, one obvious place to look is New Zealand whose electors voted in 1993 to replace their FPTP system with a version of the German two-vote system (for details on this new system, see chapter 5). This vote was the product of a long process of national debate which dates from the end of the 1970s when the parliament established a Select Committee on Electoral Law whose main purpose was to assess the operation of the existing electoral system. The Committee's scope also included the right to assess the question of electoral reform. Its report in 1980 did not favour replacing FPTP with PR, but significantly this conclusion was not supported by the Labour minority on the Committee, who called for the establishment of a wide-ranging Royal Commission on electoral reform. When next in government, in 1985, the Labour Party went ahead and established such a Commission, and in its report in December 1986, the Commission recommended the replacement of FPTP with what it called a 'mixed member proportional' system, in essence the two-vote system.

It was not until 1990 when, in a 'highly disproportionate' election, Labour was flung out of office and the new National government (with 48 per cent of the vote, but 69 per cent of the seats), elected on a manifesto of reform and change, had little choice but to take on the question of electoral reform (Vowles, 1995). In 1992 an 'indicative', or non-binding, referendum was held. This consisted of two parts. In part A, voters were asked whether the current FPTP system should be retained, or replaced by another electoral system. If they rejected FPTP, in part B, they were offered a choice of four other electoral systems to choose between: a 'supplementary member system' (somewhat akin to the British Hansard's proposals of the mid-1970s, in this case with about one-quarter of seats being farmed out among the parties on the basis of their vote proportions); STV; the two-vote system, and the alternative vote system as used in Australia.

Given the general levels of disquiet about the political system (as revealed in the opinion polls) and the close attention which had been paid to the two-vote system (not least by the 1986 Royal Commission report), the results of the 1992 referendum were not that surprising in the sense that voters showed a clear desire to change towards the two-vote system. What was surprising was the size of the vote for change. Just short of 85 per cent of voters rejected the FPTP system and two-thirds of voters (65 per cent) were in favour of the two-vote system (Harris, 1992).

This result was non-binding. It triggered another referendum campaign, with the voters being offered a clear choice between the existing FPTP system and the favoured alternative of the two-vote system. This time the result would be binding. After a long, informative and somewhat heated debate, the referendum on 6 November 1993 produced a result which, while not exactly overwhelming, was certainly conclusive enough to ensure that the system would be changed. On a turnout of 83 per cent, 53.9 per cent voted for the two-vote system and 46.1 per cent voted for FPTP. Another country had moved towards PR (Harris, 1993; Vowles, 1995).

2.6 Conclusion

There is no such thing as the perfect electoral system, though some systems have certain advantages over others. The disadvantages of FPTP are clear: it produces disproportional results; smaller parties are underrepresented, and supporters of smaller parties waste their votes. FPTP does, however, also have a number of apparent advantages, particularly in terms of its promotion of single-party, stable government; the central role of constituency representation, and its much trumpeted simplicity. Yet when each of these factors is examined more closely, there is a need to attach some qualification to them.

This, in turn, raises doubts about FPTP as an appropriate system. The only way to arrive at some definitive answers to the question of whether the system should be changed is to examine the available alternatives, which is the function of the following chapters.

Note

[1] The limited vote – first proposed in parliamentary debates in the early 1830s – was designed for multi-member constituencies, where the voter was given one less vote than the number of seats to be filled. This is similar to the single non-transferable vote system which Japan used until 1994, where each voter was given one vote to elect MPs in multi-seat constituencies. The electoral systems literature generally refers to both these systems as 'semi-proportional' because there is some success in the representation of minorities.

3

MAJORITARIAN ELECTORAL SYSTEMS: SECOND BALLOT AND THE ALTERNATIVE VOTE

As we saw in the previous chapter, Sir Russell Johnston (Liberal Democrat) won the seat of Inverness, Nairn and Lochaber in the 1992 British general election with just 26 per cent of the vote. It is results like this which give the first past the post (FPTP) system a bad name. One view often expressed in political circles is that if it were possible to clear up these sorts of anomalies without 'destroying' the 'essential' character of FPTP, then the system would not receive such a bad press. The ideal compromise is said to be one where the electoral system is still easy for the average voter to understand; where it produces strong and stable government; where there still is a single MP representing a single constituency, and, in addition, where that MP enjoys the support of the majority of his or her constituents. The critical new ingredient, therefore, is that each MP is elected with an overall majority, as opposed to the situation which prevailed in the 1992 British election when only 60 per cent of MPs were elected with an overall majority of all the votes in the constituency, a not uncommon result (Punnett, 1991).

In terms of the three main features of electoral systems introduced in the previous chapter, the main point of distinction between the majoritarian systems and FPTP is over the 'electoral formula'; there are also some differences over 'ballot structure'. The electoral formula distinction may appear quite simple, but it is seen as crucial by the proponents of majoritarian systems. Instead of requiring only a *plurality* of votes (i.e. more votes than any of the other candidates but not necessarily an overall majority) in order to win the seat, a candidate must get an overall *majority* (i.e. at least 50 per cent plus one), hence the title 'majoritarian' systems.

The ballot structure distinction really only relates to the Australian majoritarian system. As we shall see, under the alternative vote, voters rank-order all the candidates on the ballot paper; in other words, the ballot structure is 'ordinal'. Things are not quite so straightforward under the French second ballot system which, as we see in section 3.1, consists essentially of two 'categoric' ballots on different polling days either a week or a fortnight apart. Both majoritarian systems share in common with FPTP a 'district magnitude' of one; the country is divided into a series of one seat constituencies. Once again, we are dealing with non-proportional electoral systems; proportionality on a seat-by-seat basis can only occur when there are multi-seat constituencies.

Majoritarian electoral systems are seen as a compromise by those people who wish to see improvements to the FPTP system, but who are not in favour of the adoption of proportional representation (PR) systems. Whether, in fact, it is correct to view majoritarian systems as a compromise is dealt with later. First, however, we need to examine the two main types of majoritarian system in use. We start, in section 3.1, with a discussion of the second ballot system used in France. Section 3.2 outlines the alternative vote system which is used for Australian lower house elections, and a variant of which has recently been proposed for Britain. The chapter concludes, in section 3.3, with an assessment of the majoritarian electoral systems.

3.1 The second ballot system

This system (also referred to as the two-ballot system, or the runoff system) is most closely associated with France, Germany and Belgium (though with multi-member constituencies) made use of second ballot systems in the last century. It is used quite widely for lower-level elections in the USA, and in some southern states even for congressional elections. Versions of it are used for presidential elections in Austria, Brazil, Chile, Columbia, Ecuador, Finland, Mali, Poland, Portugal, Russia, Ukraine, and for legislative elections in

Mali and Ukraine. Bulgaria and Hungary have incorporated it into their variant of the German two-vote system (see chapter 5). In France it was used for elections to the Chamber of Deputies from 1928–45, and was readopted by the Fifth French Republic in 1958 for legislative elections and later, when direct elections for the presidency were introduced, for presidential elections (Cole and Campbell, 1989). From time to time it has been replaced – most recently in 1986–8 by PR (also France has opted for a PR system for its Euro elections) – but it remains quintessentially a French electoral system.

As the title suggests, the central feature of this system is a second ballot, with polling taking place on two separate days. The principal objective is to increase the likelihood that the candidate elected will have an overall majority of support in the constituency, i.e. more than 50 per cent of the votes cast. Two different versions are used in France, one for legislative elections in single-seat constituencies and one for presidential elections. In both cases the first stage is deceptively like a FPTP election. The French voters simply select their preferred candidate. If a candidate receives an overall majority of the votes (such as happened in 22 per cent of cases in the 1988 French legislative elections and 12 per cent of cases in 1993 (Cole and Campbell, 1989: 191; Goldey, 1993); as, indeed, happened in 60 per cent of cases in the 1992 British election), then he or she is deemed elected and there is no need for a second ballot. Where no candidate receives an overall majority, then a second round of voting takes place one or two weeks later. This is where the two French systems vary.

In the case of legislative elections only those candidates who receive a minimum percentage of votes are allowed to proceed to the second ballot. This minimum is set at 12.5 per cent, not of those who voted, but of the registered voters.[1] In other words, in the 1993 legislative election, when 69 per cent of the electorate turned out to vote, on average candidates needed 19 per cent of the total vote in order to qualify for the second round of voting. This minimum figure is designed to reduce the number of candidates in the second ballot and therefore to increase the likelihood that the MP finally elected has an overall majority of votes. Note that it does not *guarantee* a majoritarian result. This is because there is always the possibility that more than two candidates receive 12.5 per cent of the vote in the first round – in theory anything up to seven or eight candidates could receive 12.5 per cent of the vote – and once there are more than two candidates, then there is no guarantee of a majoritarian result. Only with two candidates can such a result be guaranteed. Of course, often candidates who manage to receive the minimum percentage of votes in the first round pull out of the race anyway so as to increase the chances for a particular candidate from another party (such as when there is a coalition bargain). (Indeed, it used to be possible for candidates to enter the race for the first time in the second round. Since 1958 all candidates must have been on the first ballot to qualify.) According to Cole and Campbell (1989: 168) in the 1988 legislative elections there were nine 'triangular contests' in the second ballot. In 1993 there were fifteen triangular contests, representing 3 per cent of all constituencies (Goldey, 1993).

An unusual feature of the French electoral process is that the ballot papers are produced by the parties themselves, not by the state. There are a set of regulations which govern the style and content of the ballot paper: it should measure approximately 10cm × 15cm; it should have the candidate's name (and that of the replacement, thus avoiding the need for a by-election) and party affiliation; it can contain further information as desired, such as a party's slogan or symbol, or background on the candidate (Holliday, 1994). Each party provides its own ballot paper. To vote, the elector chooses the appropriate ballot paper of the party he or she supports, places it in the envelope provided, and drops it into the ballot box. An example of a ballot paper for one of the French green parties is provided in Figure 3.1.

The electoral rules for presidential elections are simpler. In this case, only the candidates with the highest and second highest number of votes are allowed to run in the second round; all other candidates are excluded. With only two candidates left in the race, the final result is majoritarian. Technically speaking, of course, the final result often does not actually represent a majority of the electorate because only a certain percentage actually turn out to vote and therefore it is only a majority of the voters which determines the result. This point is even more significant in the cases where the turnout is lower in the second round of voting, as happened in 1965 and 1969. For instance, in 1969 turnout dropped from 77.6 per cent in the first round to 65.5 per cent in the second. As a result General de Gaulle's 'majority' over François Mitterrand of 52.2 per cent represented, in reality, just 45.3 per cent of the French electorate.

ÉLECTIONS LÉGISLATIVES - SCRUTINS DE MARS 93

Département du NORD - 13ᵉ Circonscription

ENTENTE DES ÉCOLOGISTES
GÉNÉRATION ÉCOLOGIE - LES VERTS

Mᵐᵉ DOMINIQUE
MARTIN-FERRARI

Journaliste

Suppléant : RENAUD JOUGLET

Conseiller Municipal de Téteghem

Figure 3.1   A French legislative election ballot paper

The 1995 French presidential election result is given in Table 3.1. This provides a good example of the strategic nature of the system. On the face of it, this election was a battle between the Left and the Right, with the Socialist candidate, Lionel Jospin, taking up the mantle from the extremely unpopular François Mitterrand who was retiring from politics. Underlying this battle was an even more bitter strategic struggle between the two main candidates of the Right, the former prime minister and long-standing mayor of Paris, Jacques Chirac, and the current prime minister, Edouard Balladur, who had entered the race as favourite.

At the start of the campaign there were predictions that Jospin would be defeated in the first round, leaving the second round to be fought over by the two candidates of the Right. This was seen as a potentially dangerous scenario and one of the weaknesses of the

Table 3.1   **The 1995 French presidential election**

	First round (%)	Second round (%)
Lionel Jospin (Socialist Party)	22.3	47.4
Jacques Chirac (Rally for the Republic)	20.8	52.6
Edouard Balladur (Rally for the Republic)	18.6	
Jean-Marie Le Pen (National Front)	15.0	
Robert Hue (Communist Party)	8.6	
Arlette Laguiller (Workers' Struggle)	5.3	
Phillippe de Villiers (Another Europe)	4.7	
Dominique Voynet (Greens)	3.3	
Jacques Cheminade (Federation for a New Solidarity)	0.3	
Turnout	78.4	79.7
Invalid Votes	2.8	6.0
Valid Votes	75.6	73.7

Source: Keesing's Record of World Events.

second ballot system. If it had actually occurred, the supporters of left-of-centre parties would have been denied the right to vote for any candidate of their persuasion in the second round. In the event, and despite the fact that his campaign started late, Jospin managed to produce a dramatic recovery in the Socialist vote, and topped the poll in the first round with 23.3 per cent of the vote. Meanwhile, Chirac, who fought a blistering campaign, pushed Balladur into third place and out of the race.

In the second round, a fortnight later, Chirac emerged the victor with 52.6 per cent of the vote. It should be noted, however, that this second round election saw an unprecedented 1.9 million voters (6 per cent) who spoiled their votes. As a result, Chirac received the active support of less than half the total French electorate.

The fact that French voters are given two opportunities to declare a preference for a candidate means that, in essence, the electorate as a whole is ranking the candidates in terms of first and second choice. In this respect, the second ballot system shares some features in common with preferential systems such as the alternative vote or the single transferable vote (STV). However, there are two peculiar features of the second ballot system. First, it is unusual in that, on the second round, certain parties and candidates are disqualified from running: electoral choice is constrained; electors are forced to think and vote in categorical terms (either candidate A or candidate B). Arguably the very high number of invalid votes in the second round of the 1995 election (Table 3.1) could, in part, reflect voters' dissatisfaction with the choices available. Second, party competition is quite different than in preferential systems because the parties, knowing how their first preferences have panned out, have two weeks to regroup and design strategies to maximize their vote. As Taagepera and Shugart (1989: 22) have noted, this 'encourage[s] the formation of bargains among the parties in between rounds'.

3.2 The alternative vote system

The alternative vote electoral system was devised in the 1870s by W. R. Ware, a professor at the Massachusetts Institute of Technology. As Jack Wright (1980: 54) points out, in the debates of the late nineteenth century about Australian independence and the setting up of the federation, considerable interest had been shown in the merits of preferential voting. This interest continued into the early years of the new federation. The basic argument was that FPTP – the system first adopted – risked a situation where parties would suffer unfairly from vote splitting. This point was illustrated by a by-election in Western Australia, when a Labor candidate was elected with 35 per cent of the vote, reflecting the fact that the support of the non-Labor side was split between three other candidates. Soon after that, in 1918, what was known as preferential voting, or majority-preferential voting, was introduced for elections to the Australian House of Representatives. (In fact, the first use of the alternative vote system in Australia was in the state of Queensland in 1893.) Almost uniquely an Australian system – where it is used for federal lower house elections as well as for most state lower house legislative elections – it was also used in parts of Canada in the 1950s. The Irish Republic uses it for presidential elections and by-elections.

Although outside Australia this electoral system is usually referred to as the alternative vote, preferential voting is a more appropriate title. 'Alternative' implies an either-or system – such as the second ballot system for instance; whereas, in reality, the voters are being asked to rank order a number of candidates, 1, 2, 3, and so on. Indeed, in Australia, voters have to rank-order *all* the candidates on the ballot paper; otherwise, their vote is declared invalid. An example of an

BALLOT PAPER
HOUSE OF REPRESENTATIVES
WESTERN AUSTRALIA

ELECTORAL DIVISION OF
MOORE

Number the boxes from 1 to 5 in the order of your choice.

☐ LLOYD, Alan R
AUSTRALIAN DEMOCRATS

☐ WATSON, Mark
GREY POWER

☐ FILING, Paul
LIBERAL

☐ STEELS, Brian
THE GREENS (W.A.)

☐ BLANCHARD, Allen
AUSTRALIAN LABOR PARTY (ALP)

Remember...number <u>every</u> box to make your vote count.

Australian Electoral Commission /AEC

Figure 3.2   An Australian alternative vote ballot paper

Australian ballot paper is provided in Figure 3.2 for the electoral division (i.e. constituency) of Moore. In essence very similar to a standard FPTP ballot paper, the big difference is that voters vote in order of preference for all the candidates, in this case all five. (Note the non-alphabetical ordering of candidates names; the parties determine the order of the candidates.)

Table 3.2 provides an illustration of how the alternative vote system can produce a result quite different from one obtained in Britain. In the Hume division of New South Wales in the 1993 Australian federal elections, there were five candidates running for one seat, with 71,248 valid votes. The first count consisted of the sorting of the ballot papers in order of the first preference votes. Under FPTP, Phil Archer (Labor Party) would have been elected as the candidate with the most votes (a respectable 42 per cent of the valid vote, as compared to 34 per cent for his nearest rival, John Sharp of the National Party). However, under the alternative vote system, a candidate must receive more than 50 per cent of the vote (i.e. at least 35,625 votes in this case). Therefore, the weakest candidate, Ian Buchanan (Australian Democrats; 1,824 votes) was eliminated and his ballot papers were re-sorted according to the second preferences.

Note how more of Buchanan's votes transferred to Archer than to Sharp. This reflects the relatively close relationship between the Australian Democrats and the Labor Party (Bean *et al.*, 1990; Marks and Bean, 1992). The result of this second count was inconclusive; none of the candidates had an overall majority. The third count, therefore, consisted of the elimination of the weakest candidate – this time Dave Cox (Independent; 2,892 votes). Again more of his preferences transferred to Labor than to the other parties, and as a result, Phil Archer was still ahead of his nearest rival, John Sharp, and the margin separating them had increased. Archer now had 45 per cent of the vote (31,940 votes; a gain of 3 per cent since the first count); Sharp had 35 per cent (25,070 votes; a gain of just 1 per cent). The only other candidate remaining in the race was Stephen Ward (Liberal Party) with 14,213 votes.

The fourth, and final count, consisted of Ward's elimination and the transfer of his 14,213 votes between Archer and Sharp. Since only two candidates were left in the race this meant that one of them had to be elected in this round; one of them had to get an overall majority. Despite the fact that Archer had been leading from the outset, the

Table 3.2 An alternative vote election result: division of Hume (New South Wales) in the 1993 Australian federal elections

	Count one	Next count	Count two	Next count	Count three	Next count	Count four
Dave Cox (IND)	2,028	+864	2,892 eliminated				
Ian Buchanan (Democrats)	1,824 eliminated						
Phil Archer (Labor)	29,773	+562	30,335	+1,605	31,940	+1,035	32,975
Stephen Ward (Liberals)	13,681	+140	13,821	+392	14,213 eliminated		
John Sharp (National)	23,942	+256	24,198	+872	25,070	+13,174	38,244 elected
Non-transferable		2		23		4	

Source: Australian Electoral Commission (1993).

final victory went to Sharp, who received 93 per cent of Ward's transfers, giving him a final vote tally of 38,244 (54 per cent) as against 32,975 votes (46 per cent) for Archer. The huge transfer from Ward to Sharp was due to the fact that the Liberal and National parties work closely together in a coalition arrangement, whether in government or opposition, and so their supporters are actively encouraged to transfer votes between the two parties (McAllister, 1992).

At first glance, the alternative vote system certainly seems fairer than any of the other systems considered so far. Unlike FPTP (and, in some circumstances, second ballot), the candidate elected has more votes than all the other candidates combined; he or she enjoys majority support in the constituency. This system also allows the voters a greater say over who they want to represent them: if it is not to be their first choice, then they can choose a second. Arguably there is a third advantage of this system over the second ballot system. Because the voting takes place on one day, there is no possibility for the parties to adopt manipulative strategies to try and maximize their gains; there is no second round of voting a fortnight later.

Whether in fact this is a fairer system than FPTP is not as clear as might at first appear. For instance, under the Australian electoral rules, a voter must vote for all the candidates on the ballot paper (though some exceptions are allowed, as shown by the twenty-nine non-transferable votes in Table 3.2). Such a requirement is peculiar to Australia, and it is one major reason for the higher number of invalid votes in Australia than elsewhere (Farrell *et al.*, 1996; McAllister and Makkai, 1993). Whether the requirement to complete all the preferences produces a 'more democratic' result is debatable. It adds considerable burden to the vote process and has opened the way for the party machines to make use of 'how to vote' cards to direct voters on how to complete preferences. Arguably it diminishes the whole point of preferential voting if the order of preferences is pretty much determined in advance by party strategists (Farrell *et al.*, 1996; Wright, 1986).

There is no particular reason why another country adopting the alternative vote system should incorporate such a rule. However, this would then open the possibility of large numbers of non-transferable votes, in some cases resulting in the candidate finally elected not actually having the support of the majority of voters. In any event, there are still a large number of wasted votes under the Australian system; 46 per cent of those who voted in the Hume division in 1993 did not support the winning candidate. In common with the second ballot and the FPTP systems, a large proportion of voters remain unrepresented.

3.3 Is the majoritarian electoral system appropriate for Britain?

Would a majoritarian electoral system deal adequately with the apparent problems of the current FPTP system in Britain? One way to assess this is to examine the record of the existing systems in Australia and France. In the concluding chapter we assess the question of relative proportionality of the various electoral systems in a systematic manner, but we can already obtain some impressions of how 'fair' they are by examining election results over time in the two countries.

Tables 3.3 and 3.4 present percentages of votes, seats and vote–seat differences in both countries in post-war elections (since 1962 in France, the first election held under the Fifth Republic). These tables provide easy comparisons with the trends in British elections which we saw in the previous chapter (Table 2.1). Overall, when drawing comparisons between FPTP and the two majoritarian systems, the trends are strikingly similar. Table 3.3 reveals a systematic bias in the French system against the parties on the two extremes, reflecting the tendency – in the second ballot – for voters to gravitate towards the centre as the candidates of the extreme parties (more usually the Communists or the National Front) are excluded. The 1993 election was particularly interesting in this regard. For instance, despite having its highest ever vote, the National Front (with 12.7 percent of the vote) ended up without any seats. Note also how in this election the two mainstream parties of the Right, the Gaullists and the Union for French Democracy (UDF), both benefited from very high vote–seat distortions in their favour (the Gaullists' seat percentage was twenty-four points higher than their share of the vote; for the UDF the difference was thirty-seven points), while the Socialists had 9 per cent fewer seats than their share of the vote. The single exception to this trend was in 1986 when a PR electoral system was used. Note how in this case the percentage variations between votes and seats were

Table 3.3 French legislative elections, 1962–93: vote and seat percentages

	Socialist Party[a]			Communist Party			Gaullists		
	Vote (%)	Seat (%)	Diff. (%)	Vote (%)	Seat (%)	Diff. (%)	Vote (%)	Seat (%)	Diff. (%)
1962	19.8	22.5	+2.7	21.9	8.8	−13.1	33.7	49.5	+15.8
1967	18.9	25.1	+6.2	22.5	15.3	−7.2	33.0	40.6	+7.6
1968	16.5	12.1	−4.4	20.0	7.0	−13.0	38.0	60.0	+22.0
1973	19.1	18.8	−0.3	21.4	15.4	−6.0	26.0	37.6	+11.6
1978	22.8	21.5	−1.3	20.6	18.1	−2.5	22.8	30.0	+7.2
1981	36.6	56.5	+19.9	16.1	9.2	−6.9	21.2	16.9	−4.3
1986[b]	31.3	35.6	+4.3	9.7	5.8	−3.9	26.8	26.3	−0.5
1988	36.6	46.8	+10.2	11.2	4.3	−6.9	19.1	22.2	+3.1
1993	19.1	9.9	−9.2	9.1	4.0	−5.1	20.2	44.5	+24.3

	Union for French Democracy			National Front		
	Vote (%)	Seat (%)	Diff. (%)	Vote (%)	Seat (%)	Diff. (%)
1978	22.0	26.2	+4.2	0.3	0.0	−0.3
1981	18.9	12.4	−6.5	0.2	0.0	−0.2
1986[b]	15.8	23.0	+7.2	9.8	6.3	−3.5
1988	18.6	23.4	+4.8	9.8	0.2	−9.6
1993	19.6	37.3	+17.7	12.7	0.0	−12.7

Notes: Percentages do not add to 100 because not all parties have been included.
[a] Including Radical Socialist Party from 1962–8.
[b] PR election in 1986.
Sources: Mackie and Rose (1991); Godley (1993); Ysmal (1994).

Table 3.4 **Australian House of Representatives elections, 1949–96: vote and seat percentages**

	Labor Party[a]			Liberals			Country/National		
	Vote (%)	Seat (%)	Diff. (%)	Vote (%)	Seat (%)	Diff. (%)	Vote (%)	Seat (%)	Diff. (%)
1949	46.0	38.8	−7.2	39.4	45.5	+6.1	10.9	15.7	+4.8
1951	47.6	43.0	−4.6	40.6	43.0	+2.4	9.7	14.0	+4.3
1954	50.0	47.1	−2.9	38.6	38.8	+0.2	8.5	14.1	+5.6
1955	44.6	38.5	−6.1	39.7	46.7	+7.0	7.9	14.8	+6.9
1958	42.8	36.9	−5.9	37.2	47.5	+10.3	9.3	15.6	+6.3
1961	47.9	49.2	+1.3	33.6	36.9	+3.3	8.5	13.9	+5.4
1963	45.5	41.0	−4.5	37.1	42.6	+5.5	8.9	16.4	+7.5
1966	40.0	33.3	−6.7	40.2	49.6	+9.4	9.7	16.3	+6.6
1969	47.0	47.2	+0.2	34.8	36.8	+2.0	8.6	16.0	+7.4
1972	49.6	53.6	+4.0	32.1	30.4	−1.7	9.4	16.0	+6.6
1974	49.3	52.0	+2.7	34.9	31.5	−3.4	10.8	16.5	+5.7
1975	42.8	28.4	−14.4	41.8	53.5	+11.7	11.3	18.1	+6.8
1977	39.6	30.7	−8.9	38.1	54.0	+15.9	10.0	15.3	+5.3
1980	45.1	40.8	−4.3	37.4	43.2	+5.8	8.9	16.0	+7.1
1983	49.5	60.0	+10.5	34.4	26.4	−8.0	9.2	13.6	+4.4
1984	47.5	55.4	+7.9	34.4	30.4	−4.0	10.6	14.2	+3.6
1987	45.8	58.1	+12.3	34.6	29.1	−5.5	11.5	12.8	+1.3
1990	39.4	52.7	+13.3	35.0	37.2	+2.2	8.4	9.5	+1.1
1993	44.9	54.4	+9.5	37.1	33.3	−3.8	7.2	10.9	+3.7
1996	39.2	32.4	−6.8	39.0	52.0	+13.0	8.2	12.2	+4.0

	Democratic Labor Party				Australian Democrats		
	Vote (%)	Seat (%)	Diff. (%)		Vote (%)	Seat (%)	Diff. (%)
1955	5.2	0.0	−5.2	1977	9.4	0.0	−9.4
1958	9.4	0.0	−9.4	1980	6.6	0.0	−6.6
1961	8.7	0.0	−8.7	1983	5.0	0.0	−5.0
1963	7.4	0.0	−7.4	1984	5.4	0.0	−5.4
1966	7.3	0.0	−7.3	1987	6.0	0.0	−6.0
1969	6.0	0.0	−6.0	1990	11.3	0.0	−11.3
1972	5.2	0.0	−5.2	1993	3.8	0.0	−3.8
1974	1.4	0.0	−1.4	1996	6.7	0.0	−6.7
1975	1.3	0.0	−1.3				
1977	1.4	0.0	−1.4				
1980	0.3	0.0	−0.3				

Notes: Percentages do not add to 100 because not all parties are included.
Sources: Mackerras (1996); election results.

much smaller across the board, and how the smaller parties tended to fare much better, particularly the extremist National Front.

In Australia, smaller parties (the Democratic Labor Party and the Democrats) have never managed to win a seat (Table 3.4), even though in some cases they have more votes than the British Liberal Party which *does* win seats under FPTP. This indicates how majoritarian systems can, and do, produce results which are even more inequitable than FPTP. The interesting case to note here is the National Party which consistently benefits from more seats than its relatively small vote warrants. This reflects the fact that, as a farmer's party, its vote is geographically focused in agricultural areas (McAllister, 1992). Just as with FPTP in Britain, a party benefits greatly from a large geographical concentration in its vote.

Apart from the unfair treatment of smaller parties, the majoritarian systems can also produce anomalous majorities, similar to those we saw with FPTP in the previous chapter. For instance, in eight of the twenty Australian elections in Table 3.4 (i.e. in 1949, 1955, 1958, 1963, 1975, 1977, 1980, 1996), the Liberal Party was awarded more seats than the Labor Party despite having won fewer votes. For a period, from 1983–93, there was a systematic bias in the seats-to-votes ratio for the governing Labor Party – a trend which bears a marked resemblance to that of the British Conservatives under FPTP (see Table 2.1). This helps to explain the dominance of the Labor Party in Australian politics over the past decade or so, a dominance which was shattered in 1996 (and when, for the first time in a decade, the party was awarded a lower share of seats than its vote warranted). In conclusion, the evidence from both majoritarian systems suggests electoral trends which are strikingly similar to those for FPTP. Smaller parties are disadvantaged; larger parties are advantaged; parties with a good geographical concentration in support tend to do better, and governments with a majority of seats are the norm.

A second way of assessing the merits of majoritarian electoral systems is to test them out among British voters, to see what difference they might make to an FPTP election result. In the immediate aftermath of the 1992 British general election, Patrick Dunleavy and his colleagues tested out a range of different electoral systems on a sample of almost 10,000 British voters (Dunleavy *et al.*, 1992; 1993). One of the systems tested was the alternative vote. The respondents were given mock ballot papers which included the names of real party candidates to fill out. The idea was to replicate the

British election in the same constituencies but using a different electoral system.

Table 3.5 shows the comparison between the actual (FPTP) 1992 result and what might have been the result had the alternative vote electoral system been used. As would be expected, there is little improvement in the overall proportionality of the result: the larger parties continue to win more seats proportionate to votes, the smaller parties continue to win fewer; the Liberal Democrats in particular remain grossly underrepresented. As Dunleavy *et al.* comment (1992: 5): 'The most striking impression from these results is of how little difference the alternative vote would make ... The Conservative majority in the House of Commons would disappear, but they would be only one seat short of overall control and would be certain still to form the government.' These findings are consistent with an earlier study by Denver and Hands who suggested that 'the major parties have little to fear from a modest move in the direction of electoral reform which is all that the alternative vote represents' (1989: 27).

The research by Dunleavy and his colleagues reveals some interesting trends about British party support under the alternative vote electoral system. For instance, they found that, when allowed the choice, one in ten Liberal Democrat voters actually gave their first preference vote to another party. The supporters of the larger parties tended to be more loyal. As for what the voters did with their second preference votes, Table 3.6 suggests two distinct patterns. In the case of supporters of the two large parties, there is a far greater tendency to vote only for their party and not to transfer their votes to any other party (a quarter of them declared no second preference). And of those who did declare a second preference, the bulk of them (more than half in each case) transferred votes to the Liberal Democrats. This stands to reason as we would expect voters to gravitate towards the centre.

By contrast, in the case of supporters of the smaller British parties, far more of them are prepared to declare a second preference and, when they do so, they have a greater tendency to spread the vote across two or more parties (e.g. note how the second preference vote of Liberal Democrat supporters divides evenly between the Conservatives and Labour). On this latter point, Dunleavy *et al.* (1993: 184) suggest that 'British voters receive much more political information about the Conservative and Labour parties than about rival parties. Hence it is inherently easier for ''minor'' party voters to form

Table 3.5 Parties' seats in the UK under alternative vote compared with the 1992 FPTP election result: the Rowntree/ICM survey

	No. of seats	Alternative vote result				FPTP 1992 result			
		Con.	Lab.	LD	Other	Con.	Lab.	LD	Other
South	261	203	44	14	0	209	45	7	0
North and Midlands	263	114	146	3	0	110	150	3	0
Scotland	72	5	52	9	6	11	49	9	3
Wales	38	3	28	4	3	6	27	1	4
Britain	634	325	270	30	9	336	271	20	7
Net change in seats		−11	−1	+10	+2				

Source: Derived from Dunleavy et al. (1992: Table 5).

Table 3.6 Inter-party transfers by British voters in 1992: the Rowntree/ICM survey

	First party supported				
	Conservative (%)	Labour (%)	Liberal Democrats (%)	Green (%)	Scottish/Welsh Nationalist (%)
Second party					
Conservative	—	9	38	12	12
Labour	9	—	33	31	43
Liberal Democrats	56	50	—	47	23
Green	6	11	15	—	9
Scottish/Welsh Nationalists	1	7	2	3	—
No second preference	28	23	12	7	14
(N)	(3,108)	(2,343)	(1,253)	(98)	(191)

Source: Dunleavy et al. (1992: Table 3).

multiple preferences about the "major" parties, than for "major" party voters to rank the "minor" parties.'

Of the two majoritarian systems (second ballot and alternative vote), the alternative vote has received by far the most positive coverage in the UK. From time to time it has been proposed as the best available option for electoral reform. Most recently, the *Report of the Working Party on Electoral Systems* (Labour Party, 1993) – an internal inquiry by the Labour Party, referred to as the Plant Report – recommended an adapted form of the alternative vote (which incorporates some aspects of the second ballot system) for elections to the House of Commons. Entitled the 'supplementary vote', its invention is credited to the Labour MP, Dale Campbell-Savours. The idea is that instead of voting in order of preference for all the candidates on the ballot paper, the British voter would have just two preference votes. It was proposed that there should be two columns of boxes next to the candidate names on the ballot paper, with the voter marking an 'X' in the first column next to one candidate (first preference), and another 'X' in the second column next to another candidate (second preference). Much like the presidential version of the French second ballot system, if no candidate receives at least 50 per cent of the vote in the first round of counting, then all but the top two candidates are eliminated and the second column of votes is redistributed. The candidate with the most votes (and thereby an overall majority) wins.

According to the Plant Report, the supplementary vote electoral system enjoys all the advantages of the alternative vote system – in particular that it is constituency-based and has a strong likelihood of producing majority governments. It is credited with two further advantages: first, that it is simple to understand, and second, 'that it avoids the counting of "weak" preferences, because only first and second choices would be registered by voters, and only the candidates who came first or second on the first count would be included on the second count, should one be needed. Thus, it does not allow a third-placed candidate to come through the middle' (Labour Party, 1993: 20). Dunleavy *et al.* (1992) are not so sure on the second point. In their analysis they could find only one constituency where the result would be different if the supplementary vote were used instead of the alternative vote. They do agree, however, that the supplementary vote would be far easier for British voters to understand. In chapter 7 we will assess the relevance of this latter point. After all, why should

British voters be so different from their counterparts elsewhere that they require a 'simple' electoral system? (For further criticism of the Plant Report, see Norris, 1995.)

A final point in assessing the two majoritarian systems is raised by Douglas Rae who argues that neither system is 'unalloyed' i.e. neither is really a majoritarian system. The second ballot system used for French legislative elections does not ensure a majoritarian result unless just two candidates are left in the second round, and even if only two candidates remain (and we can include the presidential system here), there is some question over whether the final result is majoritarian. Fewer people may turn out to vote in the second round, and voter choice has been reduced. There are also problems with the alternative vote which, Rae argues, is not 'the exact equivalent of majority rule, since votes are not to be equated with voters' (Rae, 1967: 24). For instance, as was discussed above, a high number of non-transferable votes may mean that the successful candidate is elected with less than an overall majority of the votes cast.

3.4 Conclusion

The majoritarian electoral systems have their supporters. We have seen how much of the British debate on electoral reform has tended to focus on the attributes of the alternative vote, proposing it (or some variant) as a suitable replacement for FPTP. Some of the leading scholars on electoral systems have also declared a preference for the second ballot system. In his recent study on *Comparative Constitutional Engineering*, the eminent Italian political scientist, Giovanni Sartori (1994), promotes the second ballot (or 'double ballot' as he calls it) as the best available electoral system on the grounds that it allows voters to *re-vote*: 'All other electoral systems are one-shot; the double ballot, and the double ballot only, is a two-shot system. With one shot the voter shoots very much in the dark; with two shots he or she shoots, the second time, in full daylight' (Sartori, 1994: 63; also Blais and Massicotte, 1996).

The majoritarian electoral systems – particularly the alternative vote – have a great appeal to British electoral engineers. These systems maintain the tradition of constituency representation, with single-seats. The two countries best-known for using these systems, Australia and France (Fifth Republic), have good records of stable government, incorporating strong parliamentary majorities (although the same cannot be said of France's earlier experiences with the second ballot system from 1928–45). There is little scope for voter confusion: both the second ballot and the alternative vote systems are easy to use and easy to understand. While the Australian practice of requiring that voters turn out and complete all vote preferences may add to the burden of voting, there is no reason why such rules need to be incorporated in any such system in the UK – certainly the 'supplementary vote' system proposed by the Plant Report does not.

If the majoritarian electoral systems share the positive features of FPTP, they also share most of the negative features. Smaller parties are disadvantaged, certainly small parties which lack geographic concentrations in their support bases. For the same reasons as apply under FPTP, it is questionable how 'fair' such systems are to smaller parties and to the supporters of smaller parties. These issues can only be resolved by a move towards some form of PR. However, as we shall see in the following chapters, the introduction of PR cannot be achieved without some costs of its own.

Note

[1] The minimum of 12.5 per cent was set in 1978. Between 1962–78, it was 10 per cent; between 1958–62 it was just 5 per cent.

4

THE LIST SYSTEMS OF PROPORTIONAL REPRESENTATION

The electoral systems which we have looked at so far (together with the single transferable vote (STV) system discussed in chapter 6) share a number of features in common. First, they are constituency-based, i.e. the country is divided into a series of geographically-defined constituencies, each represented by one MP (or, in the case of STV, several MPs). Second, and related, voting is candidate-based, not party-based, i.e. voters choose between the candidates put forward by the parties. In other words, these systems can be characterized as consisting of the 'direct' election of MPs rather than their 'indirect' election via party lists. A third factor which many of the systems share in common is that, for the most part, they are associated with Anglo-American countries.

In this chapter we deal with the most commonly used family of electoral systems, the list systems of proportional representation (PR), which are used in all European countries apart from Britain, France and Ireland, and which have been adopted by all newly democratizing countries. One point must be stressed at the outset. There is no single list system; there are considerable variations in the different types of list system. The most significant difference is between pure list and what is usually referred to as the additional member variant. For this reason the additional member (or 'two-vote') system is dealt with in a separate chapter.

The basic principle behind the list systems is simple enough. Each party draws up a list of candidates in each constituency. The size of the lists is based on the number of seats to be filled. In its most basic form, voters vote for parties instead of candidates (though see section 4.4). The proportion of votes each party receives determines the number of seats it can fill. For example, in the 1992 British general election, the three main parties won the following proportions of votes:

Conservatives	41.9 per cent
Labour	34.4 per cent
Liberal Democrats	17.8 per cent

If we imagine for a moment that the electoral system being used was a pure form of list PR – with the whole of the UK being treated as one vast constituency and with minimal distortion to proportionality – this would have resulted in the following distribution of seats:

Conservatives	273 seats (41.9 per cent)
Labour	224 seats (34.4 per cent)
Liberal Democrats	116 seats (17.8 per cent)

This is strikingly different from the actual seat distribution:

Conservatives	336 seats (51.6 per cent)
Labour	271 seats (41.6 per cent)
Liberal Democrats	20 seats (3.1 per cent)

As no party would have an overall majority, the result would have been the formation of a coalition government. Obviously, this is a hypothetical example and, in fact – as we shall see – in no case is such a degree of complete proportionality ever actually achieved. The list systems of PR incorporate their own distortions to proportionality. As we shall see below, this is primarily due to the fact that list systems tend to use sub-national constituencies and to the inevitable distorting effects of all electoral formulae.

The chapter begins, in section 4.1, with a brief discussion of the origins of the various list systems. This is followed by three sections which examine the mechanics of these systems according to electoral formula (4.2), district magnitude (4.3) and ballot structure (4.4). Finally, in section 4.5, we assess the operation of list systems and their consequences.

4.1 The origins of PR list systems

The origins of PR list is associated with four people in particular: Thomas Hare (England), Victor d'Hondt (Belgium), Eduard Hagenbach-Bischoff (Switzerland) and A. Sainte-Laguë (France). As we shall see, a number of the features of the contemporary list systems are named after these individuals, but it would be a mistake to give them all the credit. The origins of list systems coincided with the development of representative democracy, and particularly with suffrage extension and the development of mass parties.

From the first steps in the development of electoral systems Britain differed from its continental European neighbours, many of whom at an early stage had adopted majoritarian electoral systems involving two-ballot or multi-ballot elections. For the most part, this was in single-seat constituencies, though in Belgium, Luxembourg and Switzerland the constituencies were multi-seat. Only Denmark, Finland and Sweden did not pass through this interim phase of using majoritarian electoral systems. The move towards majoritarian electoral systems represented a clear attempt to avoid a situation where MPs could be elected without an overall majority of support in their constituencies. However, it soon became evident that this was not sufficient to prevent disproportional results at the national level. The earliest pressures for electoral reform in favour of proportional representation were felt in Belgium and Switzerland in the late nineteenth century. In both cases, as 'divided societies' (with ethnic and religious divisions), there was a desire to adopt an electoral system which could equalize the representation of the different communities involved.

Societies pressuring for electoral reform were formed: in Switzerland (the Association Réformiste de Genève) in 1865, and in Belgium (the Association Réformiste pour l'Adoption de la Représentation Proportionnelle) in 1881 (Victor d'Hondt was one of the founders). The efforts of these groups culminated in a conference at Antwerp in 1885 at which the relative merits of electoral systems recently devised by Thomas Hare (STV) and Victor d'Hondt (list PR) were discussed. D'Hondt's proposal for a list system of election was chosen as the most appropriate method. Given the absence from the conference of any representative of the British PR Society, such a conclusion was probably inevitable. Subsequently, in 1899, Belgium became the first country to adopt a list system of PR. This was the d'Hondt system, designed appropriately by a Belgian national. Finland became the next country to adopt PR in 1906, followed by Sweden in 1907. By 1920 most continental European countries had switched to a list system. As we see next, however, from there on the story becomes more complex.

4.2 Electoral formulae: largest remainders and highest averages

There are considerable variations between the different types of list system in use. It is beyond the scope of this book to attempt a comprehensive overview of all the different systems (see Carstairs, 1980; Hand *et al.*, 1979; Lijphart, 1994). The basic point of distinction is between one set of systems which determines seat allocation by *subtraction*, and another set which does so by *division*. The former is technically referred to as the 'largest remainder' systems which operate with the use of an electoral quota. Different types of quota are possible. The most common are the Hare, Droop and Imperiali quotas. List systems which operate with divisors are referred to technically as the 'highest average' systems. There are two types of highest average system in use: the d'Hondt method which is by far the most common (in the USA this is referred to as the Jefferson method), and the modified Sainte-Laguë method which is associated most with Scandinavian countries. The best way to grasp the variations between the two sets of list systems is to make use of hypothetical examples.

The **largest remainder system** is used in Austria, Belgium, Denmark (for upper-tier allocations), Greece and Iceland; Italy formerly used it for lower house elections. The central feature of this system (referred to in the USA as the Hamilton method) is an electoral quota. The counting process occurs in two rounds. In the first round, parties with votes exceeding the quota are awarded seats, and the quota is subtracted from their total vote. In the second round, those parties left with the greatest number of votes (the 'largest remainder') are awarded the remaining seats in order of vote size. This counting process is shown by the example in Table 4.1. Here we have five parties running for five seats. The total valid vote is 1,000 votes. In this example we make use of the Hare quota which is the most commonly used. This is often referred to as the 'simple quota'

Table 4.1   **A hypothetical example of the operation of the largest remainder system**

Total valid vote = 1000
Number of seats = 5
Hare quota = 1000/5 = 200

	First round votes	Hare quota	Seats	Second round remainder	Seats	Total seats
Conservatives	360	200	1	160	1	2
Labour	310	200	1	110	0	1
Liberal Democrats	150	—	0	150	1	1
Green Party	120	—	0	120	1	1
Raving Loonies	60	—	0	60	0	0

and is used in Austria and Belgium at the constituency level, and in Denmark and Greece (and formerly Italy) for higher-tier seat allocation (see below, pp. 69–70). The Hare quota is calculated as follows: total valid vote divided by the number of seats, or $1000 \div 5 = 200$.

The first stage of the counting process consists of sorting the votes into different piles for each of the parties. Here we see that both the votes received by the Conservatives (360 votes) and Labour (310 votes) exceed the quota (200 votes), and therefore each is awarded one seat in the first round. Next, the quota is subtracted from the Conservative and Labour totals, resulting in the following distribution of remaining votes: Conservatives, 160; Liberal Democrats, 150; Greens, 120; Labour, 110; Raving Loonies, sixty. Since three more seats remain to be filled, these are awarded to the parties with the largest remaining votes: Conservatives, Liberal Democrats and Greens. The final result, therefore, is two seats for the Conservatives, and one each for Labour, Liberal Democrats and Greens.

As the example suggests, the largest remainder system produces proportional results; smaller parties have an easier task in winning seats than they would in the systems discussed in the previous chapters. In this case the Green Party won the same number of seats as Labour despite having barely a third of the vote. The largest remainder system, therefore, tends to favour the smaller parties, especially when using the Hare quota. The relative importance of remainders in the allocation of seats can be reduced by using a lower quota, thereby making it more difficult for smaller parties to win seats. Two alternative quotas are used in some cases, the Droop quota (often referred to as the Hagenbach-Bischoff quota) and the Imperiali quota. The Droop quota (which is used in Greece) will be discussed in detail in chapter 6. It is calculated by dividing the total valid vote by the number of seats plus one, adding one to the result and ignoring fractions. The Imperiali quota (which was used in Italy until 1993) is calculated by dividing the total valid vote by the number of seats plus two. As the following example shows – using the figures from Table 4.1 – these different formulae produce progressively smaller quotas:

Hare:	votes ÷ seats	1000 ÷ 5	= 200
Droop	[votes ÷ seats + 1] + 1	[1000 ÷ 5 + 1] + 1	= 167
Imperiali	votes ÷ seats + 2	1000 ÷ 5 + 2	= 143

Lower quotas result in more seats being allocated to parties receiving a full quota and fewer being allocated by remainders, and therefore somewhat less proportional results. If the example in Table 4.1 is recalculated using the Imperiali quota instead of the Hare quota, this produces quite a different result. Since the Conservatives and Labour now qualify for two quota seats each, and the Liberal Democrats for one quota seat, this means that all five seats are filled in the first round, without any need to take account of remainders. The final tally is two seats each for the Conservatives and Labour, and one seat for the Liberal Democrats. The Green Party does not win a seat.

The **highest average system** is far more common than the largest remainder system. Instead of using a quota, it operates according to a divisor method. The system derives its name from the method by which seats are allocated to the parties. Each party's votes are divided by a series of divisors to produce an average vote. The party with the 'highest average' vote after each stage of the process wins a seat, and its vote is then divided by the next divisor. The process is continued until all the seats have been filled. Two main types of divisor are in operation: the d'Hondt system (with the divisors, 1, 2, 3, 4, etc.; used in Finland, Israel, Luxembourg, the Netherlands, Portugal, Spain and Switzerland) and the modified Sainte-Laguë system (with the divisors, 1.4, 3, 5, 7, etc.; used in Denmark, Norway and Sweden).[1]

Table 4.2 presents the election results for the same hypothetical example as above, this time using the d'Hondt highest average system. The counting process is quite simple. First, the votes are sorted into piles for each of the parties. These totals are then divided by the d'Hondt divisors, 1, 2, 3, and so on until all the seats have been allocated. The seats are awarded to those parties with the highest averages. Because in this example it is a five-seat constituency, literally this means that we are looking for the five highest numbers in the table. The numbers in italics indicate the sequence in which the seats have been filled. The seats are allocated in the following sequence:

First seat	360 votes	Conservative
Second seat	310 votes	Labour
Third seat	180 votes	Conservative
Fourth seat	155 votes	Labour
Fifth seat	150 votes	Liberal Democrat

While this result is more proportional than under FPTP or majoritarian systems – in the sense that smaller parties like the Liberal Democrats have a chance of winning seats – it should be noted that this is a less proportional result than was achieved in the largest remainder example in Table 4.1; the Green Party does not win a seat. This result is consistent with the argument that d'Hondt is one of the least proportional of the list electoral formulae (Lijphart, 1994). This point will be explored in chapter 7 when we deal with the question of proportionality of electoral systems.

A much more proportional result can be achieved by replacing the d'Hondt divisors of 1, 2, 3, 4, etc. with the odd-integer divisor series, 1, 3, 5, 7, etc. This is known as the pure Sainte-Laguë system (in the USA it is known as the Webster method), and according to Lijphart (1994: 23) it 'approximates proportionality very closely and treats large and small parties in a perfectly even-handed way'. This system is not currently in use anywhere – though New Zealand recently adopted it in its 1993 referendum – largely because it is seen as 'too proportional'. Instead, the practice has been to modify the first integer, replacing 1 with 1.4. This reduces the overall proportionality making it more difficult for small parties to win seats. According to Lijphart, as a result, modified Sainte-Laguë lies on a scale of proportionality somewhere in-between d'Hondt and pure Sainte-Laguë.

Table 4.3 shows an election count with modified Sainte-Laguë using the same hypothetical case as before. The presentation is

Table 4.2 A hypothetical example of the operation of the d'Hondt highest average system

Total valid vote = 1000
Number of seats = 5

	Conservatives	Labour	Liberal Democrats	Green Party	Raving Loonies
Base number of votes cast	360	310	150	120	60
1st rank: base number divided by 1	360 *1st seat*	310 *2nd seat*	150 *5th seat*	120	60
2nd rank: base number divided by 2	180 *3rd seat*	155 *4th seat*	75	60	30
3rd rank: base number divided by 3	120	103	50	40	20
Seats won	2	2	1	0	0

Table 4.3 A hypothetical example of the operation of the modified Sainte-Laguë highest average system

Total valid vote = 1000
Number of seats = 5

	Conservatives	Labour	Liberal Democrats	Green Party	Raving Loonies
Base number of votes cast	360	310	150	120	60
1st rank: base number divided by 1.4	257 *1st seat*	221 *2nd seat*	107 *4th seat*	85	42
2nd rank: base number divided by 3	120 *3rd seat*	103 *5th seat*	50	40	20
3rd rank: base number divided by 5	72	62	30	24	12
Seats won	2	2	1	0	0

the same as for Table 4.2, only this time the divisors are 1.4, 3, 5, etc. The result is the same, but the sequence in which the seats are allocated varies. The result is as follows:

First seat	257 votes	Conservative
Second seat	221 votes	Labour
Third seat	120 votes	Conservative
Fourth seat	107 votes	Liberal Democrats
Fifth seat	103 votes	Labour

If the election had been fought using pure Sainte-Laguë divisors (1, 3, 5, etc.), the result would have been far more proportional, namely:

First seat	360 votes	Conservatives
Second seat	310 votes	Labour
Third seat	150 votes	Liberal Democrats
Fourth seat	120 votes	Green Party
Fifth seat	120 votes	Conservatives

In summary, this section has assessed the three main electoral formulae in use in PR list systems. Comparative research shows that, separate from the effects of district magnitude, the electoral formula which produces the most proportional result is the largest remainder system with the Hare quota; modified Sainte-Laguë highest average forms an intermediate category; and the least proportional systems are d'Hondt highest average and largest remainder with the Imperiali quota (Lijphart, 1986; 1994). The fact is, however, that all these systems incorporate some element of disproportionality. This can be minimized by having a large district magnitude or by 'two-tier' seat allocations, as we see in the next section.

Disproportionality can also be reduced by the process of *apparentement*. As we have seen in the list systems, smaller parties can have a lot of 'wasted' votes, i.e. situations in which they do not have enough votes to fill seats. It can happen that a series of small parties miss winning any seats by relatively small margins. *Apparentement* refers to a situation in which parties formally agree to link their lists, i.e. where two or more parties declare that they are contesting the election as an alliance. The ballot papers are not affected; the parties still appear as separate lists. However, in the counting process all their spare votes are pooled, increasing the prospect that one of the smaller parties will succeed in having an extra candidate elected. *Apparentement* is used most commonly in d'Hondt systems (notably the Netherlands, Israel and Switzerland) to compensate for disproportionality. In the past it was also used in Scandinavian countries (Denmark, Norway and Sweden), but for the most part they stopped using it with the move towards Sainte-Laguë, and, later, modified Sainte-Laguë (Carstairs, 1980: 216–18; Lijphart, 1994: 134–7).

4.3 District magnitude: constituency size and two-tier districting

At the start of the chapter it was pointed out that the best way to maximize proportionality is to have the entire country as one vast constituency. Once we start to carve up a country into smaller constituencies an element of disproportionality is introduced. The basic relationship for all proportional systems is: the larger the constituency size (and, hence, the larger the district magnitude), the more proportional the result. This relationship is examined in detail in chapter 7 below, but the basic idea should be clear. If a country is divided up into small constituencies, there is a far greater number of voters whose votes are wasted in the counting process. For instance, depending on the different electoral formulae used in the examples in the previous section, the supporters of the Raving Loonies and sometimes also of the Green Party did not see their votes translated into seats. If that experience is repeated across the country, then there is the prospect of a lot of voters just missing the chance of having their preferred party elected in their constituency. In the aggregate, therefore, the result is disproportional.

As the size of constituencies increases, so do the prospects for a proportional result. The ideal situation – as far as proportionality is concerned – is one where the entire nation is one constituency. This is the practice in Israel and the Netherlands. In Israel all 120 members of the Knesset are elected on a national level. In theory that should mean that in order to be elected a candidate needs only 1/120th, or 0.83 per cent, of the total national vote. However, this 'pure' proportionality is reduced somewhat both by the electoral formula which is used (d'Hondt – the least proportional of the list formulae) and by the requirement that a party must win at least 1.5 per cent of the national vote to qualify for seats (legal thresholds are discussed below). The Netherlands comes closer to a purely proportional result. All 150 members of the Tweede Kamer (Second Chamber) are elected on the basis of the national distribution of party votes. A candidate needs just 1/150th, or 0.67 per cent, of the total national vote to be elected. This means that, depending on the turnout, a party can be represented in parliament with as few as 60,000 votes. In fact, it is possible for candidates to be elected with even smaller proportions. To prevent this possibility there is a minimum threshold of 0.67 per cent of the vote which a party must win in order to qualify for any seats.

The problem with national-level representation is that it reduces the contact between representatives and voters. In effect there is no such thing as a constituency politician. There is a danger that the geographical location of MPs (either by birth or residence) may be concentrated in the urban, more populated areas, leaving whole swathes of the population 'unrepresented'. One solution to this – which is the Dutch practice – is to have the party lists drawn up at the regional level. This means that even if the determination of who wins seats is determined by the national vote, at least those candidates elected will be more evenly spread across the country.

The more common practice is to divide the country up into regions or constituencies. However, these are not constituencies in the sense in which one understands them in Britain. In all cases the constituencies are larger than in the UK, and in some cases substantially so. According to Lijphart's (1994) detailed overview, the smallest average constituencies are in Greece (with about five seats), while the largest are in Portugal (with about twenty-four seats). Therefore, it is not possible to call the MPs elected under these systems 'constituency politicians' in the sense used in the UK. This point is reinforced by the fact that voters are voting for parties and not candidates, and therefore constituency representation does not feature so highly in the voting process (Katz, 1980; see also the discussion on ballot structure below).

It is possible to build into the system a means of increasing the proportionality of the result without having overly large constituencies. Technically this is referred to as 'two-tier districting', where a certain number of seat allocations are determined in a 'higher tier' such as the wider region, or even across the nation as a whole. This two-tier method irons out any discrepancies at the constituency level and produces a result which is more proportional. The basic idea is that any votes which have been 'wasted' at the first-tier – i.e. all remaining votes which have not been used to fill seats – are pooled and the distribution of the remaining seats is determined in the second-tier. This practice is followed by all the countries using the largest remainder system or the modified Sainte-Laguë highest average system. Consistent with the fact that the d'Hondt system is the least proportional of the list formulae in use, none of the countries using it bothers with a second-tier.

Two different procedures are followed: 'remainder transfer' in the largest remainder cases and 'adjustment-seats' in the modified Sainte-Laguë highest average cases (Lijphart, 1994: 32). The 'adjustment-seats' system entails a certain fixed proportion of seats which are set aside and 'awarded to the parties in the appropriate numbers to compensate them for any shortfall in the seats they won in the constituencies' (Gallagher *et al.*, 1995: 283). In Denmark and Iceland the proportion is about 20 per cent; in Sweden, 11 per cent; and in Norway, 5 per cent. In the 'remainder transfer' system the proportions of higher-tier seats are not fixed in advance, but the outcome is the same. This practice is followed in Austria, Belgium and Greece (and formerly Italy).

For all the effects on proportionality of electoral formula and district magnitude, the list systems often contain features which give an in-built advantage to larger parties. It is common for the electoral law to include a legal threshold below which parties are not awarded any seats. In other words, this is a cutoff point which is designed to reduce the number of tiny, splinter parties in the system. The best-known example of such a legal threshold is in Germany where a party must win at least 5 per cent of the list vote (or – even more difficult – win three constituency seats) before it can be awarded any seats. In 1987, for instance, the German Green Party won 8.3 per cent of the vote which translated into forty-two (or 8.5 per cent) seats. In the 1990 all-German election, the party won only 4.8 per cent of the vote in the western part of Germany and so lost all its seats.[2]

Legal thresholds can vary greatly in size and method of operation. As we have seen, the lowest one is used in the Netherlands where a party must get at least 0.67 per cent of the vote. In Denmark the threshold is set at 2 per cent; in Sweden it is 4 per cent, and in Poland it is 7 per cent. Some thresholds apply to the upper-tier allocation only. In these cases they are used to top-up the gains of the larger parties. In Austria a party needs only to win one constituency seat to qualify for upper-tier seats, which is not too onerous given that the average constituency has twenty seats (Gallagher *et al.*, 1995: 284).

The most controversial example of topping-up was in Greece in 1981 and 1985 with a system which was euphemistically referred to as 'reinforced PR'. A party had to win at least 17 per cent of the national vote to qualify for upper-tier allocation. This caused some marked distortions in the results, and in 1989 the restriction was dropped. Probably the most elaborate threshold rule is in the Czech Republic where a party must obtain 5 per cent of the national vote. However, if it is in coalition then this threshold is made less onerous, so that a coalition of two parties requires 7 per cent of the vote, a coalition of three requires 9 per cent, a coalition of four requires 11 per cent, and so on.

4.4 Ballot structure: closed and open lists

Ballot structure is particularly important in the case of list systems. Since the basis of the system is a vote for party, rather than for candidate, there has to be a means of determining the allocation of seats between the party candidates. In other words, once we have used the electoral formula to work out how many seats each party is to be allocated, we then need some mechanism for working out which seats are to go to which candidates. In theory this should be a very simple exercise. Each party draws up a list of candidates for the given region and the seats are allocated according to the rank-order used in the list. For instance, imagine a hypothetical situation where the Conservative Party in the region of Derbyshire (say a seven-seat constituency) has selected its seven candidates and listed them in the following order, where we can guess the reasons (in parentheses) for the rank-order:

Candidate 1 (long-standing activist; party fund-raiser)
Candidate 2 (woman)
Candidate 3 (leading industrialist)
Candidate 4 (woman)
Candidate 5 (Central Office functionary)
Candidate 6 (teacher)
Candidate 7 (son of local business owner)

If in the subsequent election the party wins three seats then the first three names on the list are awarded the seats. If the party wins

ELECCIONES A CORTES GENERALES 1989
ELECCIONS A CORTS GENERALS 1989

DIPUTADOS
DIPUTATS

CONVERGÈNCIA
I UNIÓ

BARCELONA

Doy mi voto a la candidatura presentada por:
Dono el meu vot a la candidatura presentada per:

CONVERGENCIA I UNIO
(C. i U.)

MIQUEL ROCA i JUNYENT *(C.D.C.)*
JOSEP M.ª CULLELL i NADAL *(C.D.C.)*
JOSEP M.ª TRIAS DE BES i SERRA *(C.D.C.)*
LLIBERT CUATRECASAS i MEMBRADO *(U.D.C.)*
RAFAEL HINOJOSA i LUCENA *(C.D.C.)*
MARIA EUGÈNIA CUENCA i VALERO *(C.D.C.)*
FRANCESC HOMS i FERRET *(C.D.C.)*
JORDI CASAS i BEDOS *(U.D.C.)*
LLUIS MIQUEL RECODER i MIRALLES *(C.D.C.)*
PERE BALTÀ i LLOPART *(C.D.C.)*
ANTONI CASANOVAS i BRUGAL *(C.D.C.)*
SANTIAGO MARTINEZ i SAURI *(U.D.C.)*
JOSEP NICOLÀS DE SALAS i MORENO *(C.D.C.)*
SARA BLASI i GUTIERREZ *(C.D.C.)*
MARCEL RIERA i BOU *(C.D.C.)*
IGNASI JOANIQUET i SIRVENT *(U.D.C.)*
LLUIS ARBOIX i PASTOR *(C.D.C.)*
JOAN GRAU i TARRUELL *(C.D.C.)*
JOSEP M.ª OLLER i BERENGUER *(C.D.C.)*
RAMON TOMÀS i RIBA *(U.D.C.)*
YOLANDA PIEDRA i MAÑES *(C.D.C.)*
JOAN USART i BARREDA *(C.D.C.)*
LLUIS BERTRAN i BERTRAN *(C.D.C.)*
OLGA CAMPMANY i CASAS *(U.D.C.)*
MIQUEL SÀNCHEZ i LOPEZ *(C.D.C.)*
ANA M.ª PAREDES i RODRIGUEZ *(C.D.C.)*
JOAN MASAFRET i CADEVALL *(C.D.C.)*
MARTA VIGAS i GINESTA *(U.D.C.)*
ALFONS CASAS i GASSÓ *(C.D.C.)*
JOSEP MASSÓ i PADRÓ *(C.D.C.)*
FRANCESC XAVIER MIRET i VOISIN *(C.D.C.)*
VICTOR PEIRÓ i RIUS *(U.D.C.)*

Suplentes – *Suplents*

ANA M.ª DEL VALLE i RODRIGUEZ *(C.D.C.)*
ALBERT TUBAU i GARCIA *(C.D.C.)*
MIQUEL COLL i ALENTORN *(U.D.C.)*

Figure 4.1   **Spanish PR list ballot paper**

two seats then only Candidates 1 and 2 are elected. This is referred to as a 'closed' list, or a non-preferential system. For the most part it is used in 'newer democracies', such as Argentina, Columbia, Costa Rica, Israel, Portugal, Spain, Turkey and Uruguay. It is also used in Germany for the list seats and was briefly used in France in the 1986 legislative elections. Figure 4.1 provides an example of a recent Spanish ballot paper. This is the ballot for the Convergència I Unió party, where the candidate names are listed in the rank-order set by the party. The act of voting for this party consists of basically picking up this ballot paper and dropping it into the ballot box.

It is easy to see the advantages for the party elite of such a system. They can draw up their lists in such a way so as to maximize the chances for their preferred candidates to be elected. There are clear advantages to this system wherever a party wants to increase its proportion of female MPs or, perhaps, to guarantee a minimum proportion of seats to ethnic minorities. A good example of this is provided by the first democratic election of post-apartheid South Africa in April 1994. The first past the post (FPTP) electoral system of the old regime had been replaced by list PR. As Figure 4.2. shows, the ballot paper contained party names and logos, and colour photographs of the party leaders. This was a closed list; the voter was instructed as follows: 'make your mark next to the party you choose'. Andrew Reynolds (1994: 58) observes that these 'national, and unalterable, candidate lists allowed parties to present ethnically heterogeneous groups of candidates which, it was hoped, would have cross-cutting appeal'.

There are, however, clear disadvantages to such a system. The individual voters have absolutely no say over *who* represents them. The list is drawn up by the parties and all the voter can do is select one list for one party. He or she has no say over the rank-order, apart from joining the party and trying to get involved in the internal candidate selection process. (Of course, precisely the same criticism can be levelled at FPTP, see chapter 2.)

Most of the list systems operate a more flexible, or 'open', ballot structure and are, to varying degrees, preferential systems (Katz, 1986; Marsh, 1985). The least open of these are in Austria, Belgium, the Netherlands, Norway and Sweden. Figure 4.3 provides an example of the Belgian case, where the voter has two choices. He or she may either cast a vote for one party (by ticking the relevant box under the party name) or a vote for one candidate (by ticking the relevant

PAN AFRICANIST CONGRESS OF AZANIA		PAC
SPORTS ORGANISATION FOR COLLECTIVE CONTRIBUTIONS AND EQUAL RIGHTS		SOCCER
THE KEEP IT STRAIGHT AND SIMPLE PARTY		KISS
VRYHEIDSFRONT - FREEDOM FRONT		VF-FF
WOMEN'S RIGHTS PEACE PARTY		WRPP
WORKERS' LIST PARTY		WLP
XIMOKO PROGRESSIVE PARTY		XPP
AFRICA MUSLIM PARTY		AMP
AFRICAN CHRISTIAN DEMOCRATIC PARTY		ACDP
AFRICAN DEMOCRATIC MOVEMENT		ADM
AFRICAN MODERATES CONGRESS PARTY		AMCP
AFRICAN NATIONAL CONGRESS		ANC
DEMOCRATIC PARTY DEMOKRATIESE PARTY		DP
DIKWANKWETLA PARTY OF SOUTH AFRICA		DPSA
FEDERAL PARTY		FP
LUSO - SOUTH AFRICAN PARTY		LUSAP
MINORITY FRONT		MF
NATIONAL PARTY - NASIONALE PARTY		NP
INKATHA FREEDOM PARTY - IQEMBU LENKATHA YENKULULEKO		IFP

Figure 4.2   South African PR list ballot paper

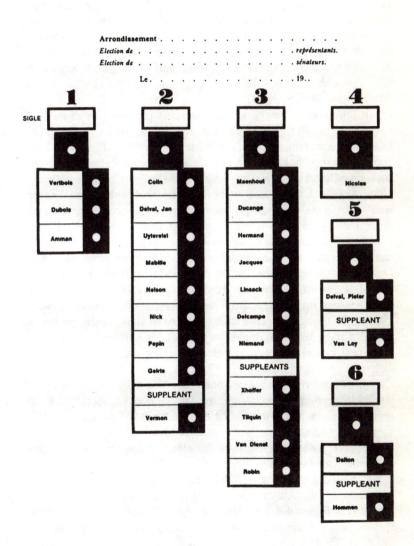

Figure 4.3 **Belgian PR list ballot paper**

box next to the candidate). In theory, placing a 'preference' next to one of the candidates has the effect of moving that candidate higher up the rank-ordering. In practice, however, if a candidate has been placed low in the rank-order to begin with, then, unless a large proportion of voters express the preferences for the same candidate, there is little chance that he or she will succeed in being elected. Research has shown that although about half of Belgian voters make use of candidate votes, only a tiny proportion of seat allocations are affected (De Winter, 1988).

An intermediate category of openness is presented by cases like Finland or Italy (before reforms in the 1990s) where 'preference' votes have a real influence on candidate rank-order. In fact, in Finland voters have no choice but to declare a preference because the vote consists of marking down the relevant code for a candidate (Katz, 1986: 88). In Italy it used to be the case that voters could either simply 'list vote' for their preferred party, or they could write down the names or numbers of up to three or four (depending on constituency size) preferred candidates under the party name. The seats were allocated to those candidates with the most personal votes. Unlike the Belgian case, in Italy 'list voting' had no effect on candidate placement. For the most part only about 30 per cent of Italian voters on average made use of preferential voting (Marsh, 1985: 368), though the percentage tended to be significantly greater in southern Italy, reflecting higher degrees of 'clientelism'. There were prominent occasions when preferential voting was seen to make a difference, for instance in the 1983 election when the porno star, 'La Ciciollina', received a huge personal vote. The Italian ballot structure tended to encourage the clientelistic and factional tendencies in the political system, and in the early 1990s the electoral law was changed so that only one personal vote could be declared. In 1993 – in the furore over political scandals – the electoral system was replaced altogether (see below and chapter 5).

Luxembourg and Switzerland operate the most flexible ballot structures of all. An example of the Luxembourg ballot paper is provided in Figure 4.4. Here the voter has as many votes as there are seats to be filled. He or she has three choices: (1) cast a 'list vote' for the party, thereby giving one preference vote to each of the party's candidates; (2) cumulate two preference votes on one candidate (as indicated by the two boxes next to each candidate's name in Figure 4.4; this option is referred to as 'cumulation'); or (3) give preferences

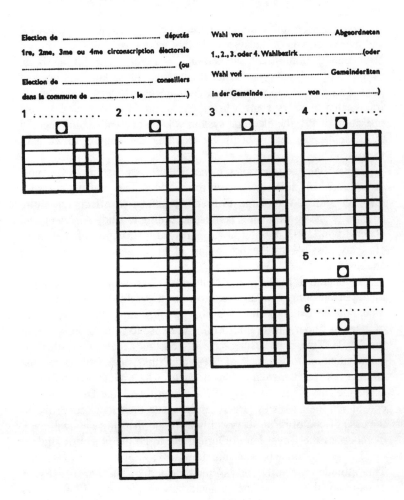

Figure 4.4   **Luxembourg PR list ballot paper**

to candidates on more than one party list. This latter option is known as *panachage*, and, according to Marsh (1985: 369), in recent elections it has been used by about 8 per cent of Swiss voters and 18 per cent of Luxembourg voters.

4.5 The operation of two list systems

As we have seen, there are a large number of countries using list PR and many variants of the system. In this section we will focus on two prominent examples, the Netherlands and Italy. The former is an example of a highly proportional system with a large number of parties represented in parliament; the latter is also a case of a highly fragmented party system where, partly due to disquiet over the operation of PR, the electoral system was first amended, and then, in 1993, replaced. Let us begin by examing the context of each of them.

As we shall see in chapter 7, the Netherlands has one of the most proportional electoral systems in the world. It uses highest averages d'Hondt with a very large district magnitude. In effect, the entire country is one constituency, so that, according to Rudy Andeweg and Galen Irwin (1993: 89), '[t]he proportional distribution of seats is as close as possible to the proportion of votes that the parties have achieved'.

The operation of PR in the Netherlands has been seen as a major factor in the long-standing tradition of successful political 'accommodation' in Dutch politics, but this has not stopped the emergence of a debate about electoral reform, which rose to some prominence in the 1980s. Two main issues have driven this debate. First, there is some attention to the lack of MP–voter links, inevitable given the absence of parliamentary constituencies. Ken Gladdish refers to academic surveys in the early 1970s which found that Dutch citizens considered their MPs as largely irrelevant to their local concerns. In the case of one of these surveys it was found that '[a]t national level, members of the Royal Family turned out to be the object of slightly more frequent contacts than individual MPs' (Gladdish, 1991: 101). This attitude of indifference is reciprocated by the Dutch MPs. A cross-national survey of parliamentarians in the early 1980s found that in 'the task of mediation between groups and individuals', British and German MPs 'scored highly'; by contrast, this activity 'was virtually ignored by the Dutch' (Gladdish, 1991: 102).

A second issue which has driven the debate about electoral reform in the Netherlands is the stability of government. This issue was brought to a head in the 1960s by the new Democrats '66 (D'66) Party which laid great stress on the inconclusiveness of Dutch elections, the length of time it took to form a government after an election and the complexity of governments which were formed. This relates to the point raised in chapter 2 about whether PR can really guarantee proper democratic accountability if the governments are formed more on the basis of post-election negotiations in smoke-filled rooms, rather than as a result of clear electoral mandates. In the Netherlands this issue was compounded by the fact that the three religious parties were always in government: new parties like D'66 were excluded.

In 1967 a parliamentary committee, known as the Cals-Donner Committee, was established to examine constitutional reform, looking into such matters as whether the Dutch should adopt a presidential system of government. Among the proposals in its 1971 report, the Cals-Donner Committee called for the replacement of nationwide PR with a system of twelve regional lists. At first this proposal seemed to carry some weight, particularly as it was endorsed by the Labour Party. However, after a long debate, the Committee's proposals were finally rejected in early 1975 and, for some time after that, little attention was given to the issue of electoral reform in the Nether-lands. Debate in recent years over the accountability of Dutch politicians to their voters has once again led to speculation about possible electoral reform, in which the Netherlands might move towards some form of two-vote system, such as used in Germany (see chapter 5). The issue is currently being considered by a parliamentary commission.

Italy has shared a great deal in common with the Netherlands, notably the high degree of proportionality of its electoral system, and the large number of parties competing for seats and ultimately winning representation in parliament. One significant difference between the two countries is that the Italians have not just talked about electoral reform; as we shall see in the next chapter, the Italians have gone ahead and radically changed their electoral system.

As one of the few political systems with a powerful second chamber, Italy used two versions of list PR. For the lower house, the Chamber of Deputies, the system was largest remainder Imperiali (with preferential voting) in thirty-two electoral districts, with a distribution of remainders through a national pool (with quota rules applying). For the Senate, the system was highest averages d'Hondt (without preference voting).

The Chamber of Deputies' ballot structure was 'open', with voters being permitted to express between three and four preferences (depending on the size of the region) on the ballot paper. To use the preference option the voters needed to know either the name or the number of the candidates (and the party they were running for) as the names were not even provided in the polling booth. As we have seen, the preference option was used only by about 30 per cent of voters on average. However, in parts of Italy the percentage was far higher, particularly in the South and the islands of Sardinia and Sicily, where candidates and parties made great efforts to try to influence the preferential vote. In some cases preferential voting was greater than 50 per cent. There were accusations that organized lobbies and even, in some cases, organized crime, played a role in trying to influence preferences in favour of their particular candidates. In 1991 a constitutional referendum was held to reduce the number of preferences allowed to just one (McCarthy, 1992).

The major reform of the Italian electoral system was in 1993 when, in the wake of a major scandal over the proprieties of the established parties and politicians, the Italians voted in a referendum to abolish list PR for the Senate. Subsequently this prompted the politicians to change also the electoral system for the Chamber of Deputies. The details of the referendum debate and the nature of the electoral reforms are long, complex and convoluted (see Donovan, 1996; Katz, 1995). The basic result is that the two houses of the legislature have ended up with electoral systems which, sharing common features, are quite distinct from each other in certain respects. The basic point of similarity is that, in each case, three-quarters of MPs are elected to represent individual constituencies, while one-quarter are elected on PR lists. However, in the case of the Senate the allocation of the list seats is based on the overall (single) vote for each party. By contrast, in the Chamber of Deputies' electoral system the voters have two separate votes, one for constituency politicians and one for party lists. In this respect, therefore, the Chamber of Deputies' system has some features in common with the two-vote system.

What have been the implications of PR for these two systems? Both have been characterized by a large number of parliamentary parties – with up to as many as fourteen parties represented in the parliament – and, in consequence, coalition governments are the norm. As we shall see in chapter 7 (see Table 7.3), in the Netherlands there have been more than seventeen changes of government since the war, while Italy has had more than twice that figure. In Tables 4.4

and 4.5 we follow the practice of the previous chapters and examine the electoral systems in terms of percentage vote–seat differences. Given the large number of parties in each system, it has been decided to present only the 'difference' figures so as to save space. The percentage votes and seats are not presented; instead, the parties have been grouped under one of three categories: large (votes greater than 9 per cent), medium (votes between 2–9 per cent) and small (votes less than 2 per cent). Furthermore, not all parties are included: many of the smaller parties are transitory and, particularly in the case of Italy, are regionally-based.

Both tables reveal very low levels of disproportionality: the difference figures are the lowest of all the electoral systems dealt with so far (and lower than the trends discussed in chapters 5 and 6). Nevertheless, there are some areas of similarity with the trends in other electoral systems. In particular the largest parties still benefit most from higher proportions of seats relative to share of votes. This is most notable in the case of the Italian Christian Democrats, demonstrating to that party the benefits of a strong geographical concentration in its support base (in the South) and explaining why it should be most resistant to change. It is also worth noting how it is only with the Christian Democrats that we see high levels of disproportionality. By contrast, there is no sign of any particular gains being made by smaller parties in the system (quite the contrary). This raises questions about just how significant a role the electoral system played in producing political instability in Italy; other factors seem to have also had a role.

The smaller the party the less beneficial the distorting effects of the electoral system. In the Netherlands we see that the record of disproportionality in the case of medium-sized parties is quite mixed; the smaller parties generally do least well (though, by contrast with FPTP, the picture for these small parties is quite rosy!). In Italy, the picture looks quite different. Here we see the smallest parties apparently having a better time of things than the medium-sized parties. There are two reasons for this. First, the Italian electoral system was less proportional and the effects of this were felt most by the medium-sized parties. Second, many of the smallest Italian parties are regionally-based and therefore benefit from a higher geographic concentration in their vote. This is particularly noticeable in the case of the South Tyrol People's Party which managed to achieve virtually perfect proportionality at each election.

Table 4.4 Differences between vote and seat percentages in the Netherlands, 1959–94

	1959	1963	1967	1971	1972	1977	1981	1982	1986	1989	1994
Large parties (average vote >9%)											
Catholic People's Party	+1.1	+1.4	+1.5	+1.5	+0.3						
Christian Democratic Appeal						+0.8	+1.2	+0.6	+1.4	+0.7	+0.5
Labour Party	+1.6	+0.7	+1.1	+1.4	+1.4	+1.5	+1.0	+0.9	+1.4	+0.8	+0.7
Liberal Party	+0.5	+0.4	-0.4	+0.4	+0.3	+0.8	—	+0.9	+0.6	+0.1	+0.8
Medium-sized parties (average vote between 2–9%)											
Anti-revolutionary Party	-0.1	—	+0.1	+0.1	+0.5						
Christian Historical Union	-0.1	+0.1	-0.1	+0.4	-0.1						
Communist Party	-0.4	-0.1	-0.3	+0.1	+0.2	-0.4	-0.1	+0.2	-0.1		
D'66			+0.2	+0.5	-0.2	-0.1	+0.2	-0.3	-0.6	+0.5	
Democratic Socialists' 70				—	-0.1	—	-0.6				
Political Reformed Party	—	-0.3	—	-0.3	—	-0.1		+0.1	-0.1	+0.1	
Radical Political Party			—	-0.5	-0.1	+0.3	—	-0.4	—		-0.4
Small parties (average vote <2%)											
Centre Party							-0.1	-0.1	-0.4		
Evangelical People's Party							-0.5	—	-0.2		
Farmer's Party	-0.7	-0.1	-0.1	-0.4	+0.1	-0.1	-0.2				
Middle Class Party				-0.2	-0.4						
Pacifist Socialist Party	-0.5	-0.3	-0.2	-0.1	-0.2	-0.2	-0.1	-0.3	-0.5		
Reformed Political Federation						-0.6	+0.1	-0.2	-0.2	-0.3	+0.2
Reformed Political Union	-0.7	—	-0.2	-0.3	-0.5	-0.3	-0.1	-0.1	-0.3	+0.1	—

Notes: The difference percentage is calculated by subtracting the percentage of seats each party was awarded from the percentage of votes it won. A positive sign indicates that the party was awarded a greater share of seats proportionate to its vote, a negative sign indicates it received a lesser share of seats, a dash indicates perfect proportionality. Not all parties are included. Blank spaces indicate that the party is no longer in existence.

Sources: Mackie and Rose (1991); election results.

Table 4.5 Differences between vote and seat percentages in Italy, 1953–92

	1953	1958	1963	1968	1972	1976	1979	1983	1987	1992
Large parties (average vote > 9%)										
Christian Democrats	+4.5	+3.4	+3.1	+3.2	+4.0	+3.0	+3.1	+2.8	+2.8	+3.0
Communist Party/Democratic Left	+1.6	-0.8	+1.0	+1.2	+1.2	+1.6	+1.5	+0.6	+1.5	+0.9
Socialist Party	—	-0.1	—	+0.1	+0.1	-0.6	—	+0.1	+0.6	+0.1
Medium-sized parties (average vote between 2–9%)										
Liberal Party	-0.8	-0.6	-0.7	-0.9	-0.6	-0.5	-0.4	-0.4	-0.4	-0.1
Radical Party						-1.1	-0.6	-0.5	-0.5	—
Republican Party	-0.8	-0.4	-0.4	-0.6	-0.7	-0.9	-0.6	-0.5	-0.4	-0.1
Social Democrats	-1.3	-0.9	-1.0	—	-0.5	-1.0	-0.5	-0.4	-0.3	-0.2
Social Movement MSI	-0.9	-0.8	-0.8	-0.6	+0.2	-0.5	-0.4	-0.1	-0.3	—
Small parties (average vote < 2%)										
Proletarian Democracy							-0.8	-0.4	-0.4	n.a.
South Tyrol People's Party		—	+0.1	—	—			—	—	n.a.
Val d'Aosta Union		+0.1	+0.1	-0.1	-0.1	-0.1		+0.1	+0.1	n.a.

Notes: The difference percentage is calculated by subtracting the percentage of votes each party was awarded from the percentage of votes it won. A positive sign indicates that the party was awarded a greater share of seats proportionate to its vote, a negative sign indicates it received a lesser share of seats, a dash indicates perfect proportionality. Not all parties are included. Blank spaces indicate that the party is no longer in existence.

Sources: Mackie and Rose (1991); election results.

4.6 Conclusion

In their various forms, the list systems of PR have proven to be the most popular with the electoral engineers, and for good reason. These systems undoubtedly give the greatest amount of control to the party headquarters, particularly in the case of closed lists where the voters have no say over which politicians are elected, but also in the case of those systems with larger district magnitudes where the average voter has little chance of knowing much about the individual candidates. List systems are also popular with many political reformers because of their greater proportionality and, in part, because, at least in theory, they allow greater scope for implementing policies to increase the representation of women and minority ethnic groupings (for further discussion, see chapter 7).

Given the prominence of the list systems generally, the fact that so many recently democratizing countries have chosen to adopt a version, the likelihood that it will eventually become the basis for the common electoral system for the European Parliament, and the fact that with very few exceptions (Italy in 1994, France in 1988) there is little sign of countries dropping this system once adopted, there is good reason for arguing that in time we could see all countries eventually adopting a version of list PR as their electoral system. History would seem to bear this out. As we have seen, in a large number of cases (the STV countries appear to be the main exceptions), countries have moved from FPTP, through some form of majoritarian system and on to list PR.

The question remains whether PR will ever be adopted as Britain's electoral system. It would appear to be a pretty safe bet to say 'very unlikely'. On each of the crucial tests of what Britain desires in its electoral system, list PR fails. First, it most definitely is not simple, though this does not appear to present any major problems for voters in those countries using it. Second, while we may be able to isolate examples of list PR countries which enjoy electoral stability (as discussed below in chapter 7), the fact is that, to most people in the UK, list PR is synonymous with electoral instability as shown by contemporary Italy, the Fourth French Republic and Weimar Germany.

Finally, for the most part, list PR systems do not incorporate a role for constituency representation (or, certainly, place far less emphasis on it than the FPTP system). More than anything else this would appear to consign list PR to the political dustbin, at least in the UK. Before reaching such a hasty conclusion, however, it is important to spend some time examining a variant of list PR which has been designed specifically to deal with the issue of constituency representation. This is a system which British policy-makers played a key role in designing and setting in place in post-war West Germany. It is a system which is currently much in vogue and, therefore, warrants a chapter all to itself.

Notes

[1] Another variant, referred to as the Hagenbach-Bischoff system, involves the use of the highest average *combined with* a quota in the first round. This is used in Belgium, Luxembourg and Switzerland. In this section, for the sake of simplicity, we will deal only with highest average without a quota.

[2] Given the unique situation of German unification, a special exception was made to the electoral law to allow the electoral threshold for parties to be calculated separately in the East and the West of the country. The Green Party won 6 per cent of the vote in the East and accordingly was allocated eight Bundestag seats (Boll and Poguntke, 1992).

5

THE TWO-VOTE SYSTEM OF PROPORTIONAL REPRESENTATION

For all the positive features of the different list systems of proportional representation (PR) reviewed in the previous chapter, the one negative point which they all share in common, at least as far as the UK debate is concerned, is the lack of constituency representation. All the other alternatives to first past the post (FPTP) – the majoritarian systems, the single transferable vote (STV) – incorporate constituency representation in some form or other and, therefore, each has its proponents. But list PR is different. To adopt a list system means giving up a tradition of 'representation' which stretches back over centuries. At the core of the Westminster tradition is the constituency politician representing the interests of voters on his or her patch of turf. The alternative of regional politicians elected on regional lists, or even (as in Israel) national politicians elected on national lists, is not viewed with much enthusiasm. The electoral system examined in this chapter is seen as offering an ideal solution because of its hybrid nature as both a first past the post system *and* a list system.

Of all the systems we have examined so far this one has had most debate about its title: 'additional member', 'compensatory PR', 'mixed member proportional', 'personalized PR', 'the German system' and 'the two-vote system'. There are problems with all of these titles. For some time the best description was probably 'the German system'. However, with the recent adoption of versions of this system by Hungary, Italy, Japan, New Zealand and Russia, and its use in Mexico, South Korea, Taiwan and Venezuela, an alternative title is required which can take account of some significant variations. The best overall title would seem to be 'the two-vote system' (Jesse, 1988). The feature which all these systems share in common is two votes: one for a constituency MP and one for a party list. The systems differ most in the following: first, in the proportion of MPs who are elected by constituency vote or list, and second, in the relationship between the constituency seats and the list seats. The latter point, as we shall see later, is crucial: in some systems the total allocation of seats is based on the number of list seats *minus* the number of constituency seats; in other systems it is based on the number of list seats *plus* the number of constituency seats.

The two-vote system has had a positive press both in Britain and elsewhere. Proposals for electoral reform (such as the Hansard Society's 1976 report) extol its virtues as a system which combines proportionality together with single-member constituency representation. It has been credited with an important role in facilitating Germany's post-war 'economic miracle'; certainly its record shines in stark contrast to the dismal instability of the inter-war Weimar Republic which operated a PR list electoral system (Pulzer, 1983). Given the fact that only Germany has a long record in using this system, the bulk of this chapter will focus on the German case. However, in section 5.3 the variations between the different two-vote systems will be assessed, while section 5.4 reports on a recent test of the two-vote system on a sample of British voters.

5.1 The operation of Germany's two-vote system

In the immediate post-war years, when Germany was divided into zones under the control of occupying powers, there was concern that any new German state which would emerge should avoid the mistakes of the Weimar period. It was the British in particular who were anxious to introduce an electoral system which would both avoid the dangers of too many parties entering the system and destabilizing it, and, at the same time, incorporate the British tradition of constituency representation. Ultimately it was the German political parties who designed the system, but the form it took was greatly influenced by British experiments in *Land* (or state) level elections in their zone

(Carstairs, 1980; Roberts, 1975). It is worth noting that even though this system is largely a post-war invention, in certain respects it does have an 'ancient lineage' (Pulzer, 1983: 104). According to Peter Pulzer, mixed constituency and list systems were proposed as early as 1914 and '[t]he nearest presentiment to the present-day system was proposed by C. H. Bornemann in 1931'.

In 1949 the electoral law for the new Federal Republic proposed that 60 per cent of MPs would be elected by FPTP in single-seat constituencies and 40 per cent elected by PR list. The lists, which were closed (i.e. the rank-ordering of candidates was determined by the parties), were drawn up on a *Land* basis. From the beginning there was a minimum threshold: a party had to win at least one constituency seat or 5 per cent of the vote in any one *Land* to qualify for list seats. In its early form, this was not a 'two-vote' system: the elector cast just one vote and this served both as the vote for the constituency candidate and for the party list of the candidate.[1]

Electoral law changes in 1953 produced the electoral system which, with only slight amendment, has been used by the German Federal Republic ever since. There were three changes in 1953. First, the 'two-vote' system was introduced: one vote, the 'primary vote' (*Erststimme*), for constituency MPs; and a 'secondary vote' (*Zweitstimme*) for the list MPs. Second, the proportion of list MPs was increased to 50 per cent. Third, the legal minimum threshold was increased, so that to qualify for list seats a party had to win at least 5 per cent of the vote in the whole federation (though there were some exemptions). There was a further change to the threshold rule in 1956 whereby parties now had to win either 5 per cent nationally or three constituency seats.

There was another temporary change to the threshold rule before the 1990 election. Given the exceptional nature of that election – occurring so soon after unification of the country – the federal court ruled that for this election the 5 per cent clause should apply separately in the two parts of the country, i.e. the western part which had formed the original Federal Republic and the recently merged eastern part which used to be the 'German Democratic Republic'. The reason for this amendment was to ensure that smaller parties which lacked suitable partners in the other part of the state would not be disadvantaged. In the event, it was the faction-ridden Green Party which was to fall foul of this clause. The West and East Green Parties did not merge before the election and therefore their respective vote totals were counted separately. The eastern Greens (*Grüne/Bündnis'90*) won 6 per cent of the vote in the eastern part of Germany, passing the 5 per cent threshold; but the western Greens won only 4.8 per cent of the vote in the western part and therefore were not eligible for any seats. As Boll and Poguntke (1992) make clear, if the two parties had merged before the election, their combined vote would have been exactly 5 per cent and they would have received considerably more seats (probably in excess of thirty) than the eight which were allotted to them on the basis of the eastern vote. Contrast this with the result for the former East German Communist Party (PDS). Its national vote was only 2.4 per cent which ordinarily would have guaranteed it no seats. However, it won 11.1 per cent of the vote in the East (just 0.3 per cent in the West) and therefore was eligible for seventeen seats under the amended rules.

In terms of the three elements of electoral systems which we have been examining throughout this book the major difference between the two-vote system and the other list systems dealt with in the previous chapter is in the area of ballot structure. As we shall see, because the list vote is so crucial to how the system operates (at least in Germany), this ensures that the large district magnitudes of the regional lists translate into highly proportional results. Indeed, whatever distortion there is in the election result is largely caused by the operation of the 5 per cent threshold. The basic point, therefore, is that in terms of average district magnitude there is nothing very unusual about the two-vote system used in Germany, nor for that matter is there anything unusual about the electoral formulae. The constituency seats are determined on the basis of FPTP (exactly as in the UK), and the list seats are determined by the largest remainder system using the Hare quota (see chapter 4, section 4.2).[2] It is in the areas of ballot structure and counting rules that the two-vote system reveals its special qualities.

The German voter has two votes for the two types of MP. In the most recent 1994 election, for instance, the Bundestag had 656 MPs: 328 (50 per cent) of these were elected to represent individual constituencies, and 328 (50 per cent) were elected from the regional lists (allocated at the *Land* level). It is important to note that the allocation of the list seats is computed on the basis of the full Bundestag membership, i.e. as if the PR list election were the whole election. In the polling station, each voter receives a ballot paper much like the one shown in Figure 5.1, and is asked to tick two

Sie haben 2 Stimmen

hier 1 Stimme
für die Wahl
eines Wahlkreisabgeordneten
(Erststimme)

hier 1 Stimme
für die Wahl
einer Landesliste (Partei)
(Zweitstimme)

1	**Dr. Kreutzmann, Heinz** Parl. Staatssekretär Borken (Hessen) **SPD** Sozialdemo- Kellerwaldstraße 7 kratische Partei Deutschlands	○	○	**SPD**	**Sozialdemokratische Partei Deutschlands** Leber, Matthofer, Jahn. Frau Dr. Timm, Zander	1
2	**Jagoda, Bernhard** Obersekretär a. D. Schwalmstadt-Treysa **CDU** Christlich Demo- Am Weißen Stein 31 kratische Union Deutschlands	○	○	**CDU**	**Christlich Demokratische Union Deutschlands** Dr Dregger, Zink, Dr Schwarz- Schilling, Frau Geier, Haase	2
3	**Wilke, Otto** Elektromeister Diemelsee-Adorf **F.D.P.** Freie Bredelarer Straße 1 Demokratische Partei	○	○	**F.D.P.**	**Freie Demokratische Partei** Mischnick, von Schoeler, Hoffie, Wurbs, Dr. Prinz zu Solms-Hohensolms-Lich	3
4	**Funk, Peter** Werkzeugmacher Baunatal 6 **DKP** Deutsche Triftweg 6 Kommunistische Partei	○	○	**DKP**	**Deutsche Kommunistische Partei** Mayer, Knopf, Frau Dr. Weber, Funk, Frau Schuster	4
5	**Keller, Gerhard** Zivildienstleistender DIE GRUNEN Frielendorf 2 Friedhofsweg 30 **GRÜNE**		○	**GRÜNE**	**DIE GRÜNEN** Frau Ibbeken, Hecker, Horacek, Kerschgens, Kuhnert	5
			○	**EAP**	**Europäische Arbeiterpartei** Frau Liebig, Haßmann, Stalleicher, Frau Kaestner, Stalla	6
			○	**KBW**	**Kommunistischer Bund Westdeutschland** Schmierer, Frau Monich, Frau Eckardt, Dresler, Lang	7
			○	**NPD**	**Nationaldemokratische Partei Deutschlands** Philipp, Brandl, Sturtz, Lauck, Bauer	8
			○	**V**	**VOLKSFRONT** Gotz, Taufertshofer, König, Riebe, Frau Weißert	9

Figure 5.1   German two-vote ballot paper

boxes: first, on the left hand side of the ballot paper for a constituency candidate, and second, on the right hand side for a regional list. The first vote is for a candidate, while the second vote is for a party.

Three points need stressing at this stage. First, the location of the different votes on the ballot paper is deliberate. The constituency vote is called the 'primary vote' (*Erststimme*); it is supposed to be more important than the list vote. However, as Taagepera and Shugart (1989: 130) point out, this is really a 'psychologically important nuance', intended to create the impression that the constituency vote is more significant. As we shall see in a moment, when considering the counting rules, 'the real impact is rather the reverse'. Second, the party list vote used in Germany is a closed (or non-preferential) list: German voters have no influence over the rank-ordering of the candidates on the party lists (short of joining a party and trying to influence the process of candidate selection). Third, since 1953 there has been no requirement for the elector to cast both votes for the same party. In the ballot paper in Figure 5.1, it is quite acceptable for a voter to mark an 'X' next to Bernhard Jagoda of the CDU and another 'X' next to the FDP. This would also be quite a rational voting strategy. As we shall see below, this practice of 'vote splitting' has become increasingly significant in German electoral behaviour.

The election count proceeds in three stages. First, there are counts in each constituency to determine which candidate is elected and to work out the total number of constituency seats for each of the parties in each of the federal *Länder*. Just like in British elections, the candidates with most votes in each constituency are elected, regardless of whether or not they have an overall majority of the votes in the constituency. In the 1994 German federal elections the distribution of first votes and seats were as follows:

	% votes	Number of seats
Christian Democratic Union (CDU)	37.2	177
Christian Social Union (CSU)	7.8	44
Social Democrats (SPD)	38.3	103
Free Democrats (FDP)	3.3	0
Green Party	6.5	0
PDS (former East German Communist Party)	4.1	4
Republicans	1.7	0

Just like all other first past the post election systems the result is highly disproportional. It is usually the case that only the two larger groupings, the Christian Democrats (CDU and CSU) and the Social Democrats, stand any chance of winning constituency seats. Indeed, this was the case from 1957–87 (Pulzer, 1983: 100). The 1990 election was unusual in that two small parties (the Free Democrats (FDP) and the former Communists) each managed to win one constituency seat, in large part as a consequence of the disruption caused by German unification. In 1994, the PDS won four constituency seats, and thereby succeeded in passing the electoral threshold (three constituency seats). In the light of this result, there have been moves to change the threshold rule to make it more difficult for the PDS to win seats, but these moves are unlikely to come to anything.

The crucial factor which separates the two-vote system from FPTP is the second vote where smaller parties have a much greater chance of winning seats. In 1994 the distribution of second votes (i.e. list votes) was as follows:

Christian Democratic Union	34.2%
Christian Social Union	7.3%
Social Democrats	36.4%
Free Democrats	6.9%
Green Party	7.3%
PDS	4.4%
Republicans	1.9%

Once the votes of parties failing to win 5 per cent of the total vote (or three constituency seats) had been excluded, the total number of seats to which each of the remaining parties was entitled was as follows:

Christian Democratic Union	244
Christian Social Union	50
Social Democrats	252
Free Democrats	47
Green Party	49
PDS	30

The first two stages in the counting process (i.e. the counting of first and second votes) are common to all existing two-vote systems. It is in the third and final stage that a very important distinction arises. The nature of this distinction is elaborated in section 5.3 below, for now we will examine how it works in the German case. The basic point of the German system is that it should produce a proportional result. In order to achieve this, it is important that the larger parties should not be overly advantaged by the greater ease with which they win constituency seats. Therefore the operating principle of this third stage in the German count is that the total number of constituency seats won by the parties should be *subtracted* from the total number of lists seats they have been allocated (and remember that the list seats are allocated at the *Land* level). It is for this reason that the two-vote system is generally referred to as the 'additional member' system, because the result of this subtraction determines the number of additional members to which each party is entitled.

Before discussing the final stage in the counting process, we need to take account of an anomaly in the German version of the two-vote system which results from the fact that constituency seats are subtracted from list seats. It is quite possible for a party to gain more constituency seats in any one *Land* than the total to which its share of the vote would entitle it. Whenever this happens the party is allowed to retain its extra seats (*Überhangmandate*, surplus mandates or bonus seats), and the size of the Bundestag is enlarged temporarily until the next election.[3] In the past, this was not a regular occurrence; up until 1990, the number of surplus mandates in any one election had never exceeded five (all for the CDU in 1961). In the 1990 election, however, there were six *Überhangmandate* seats, all won by the CDU and, as a result, the final tally of seats for the CDU increased from 262 to 268, and the membership of the 1990 Bundestag went from 656 to 662 MPs.

Überhangmandate seats proved to be decisive in the 1994 Bundestag election. In total there were sixteen *Überhangmandate* seats: four won by the Social Democrats or SPD (in Bremen and Brandenburg), and a staggering twelve won by the CDU (in Baden-Württemberg, Mecklenburg-Vorpommern, Sachsen-Anhalt, Thuringia and Saxony). This meant that what otherwise would have been a very slim Christian Democrat–Free Democrat Bundestag majority of just two seats, became in fact a relatively comfortable majority of ten seats. As Philip Cole (1995: 10) points out, this result had 'enormous political repercussions', particularly for the FDP, because '[i]f Chancellor Kohl's majority had really been only two, the smart money would have been on him ditching the FDP in a favour of a Grand Coalition with the SPD'.

In 1994 the CDU won a total of 244 seats. This included the twelve *Überhangmandate* seats. Strictly speaking, the true proportional result should have been 232 seats, i.e. 244 seats minus twelve bonus seats. In total the CDU won 177 constituency seats and was awarded sixty-seven list seats. Similarly, the SPD saw its seat total inflated by four to 252 seats (instead of 248): 103 constituency seats and 149 list seats. The CSU's seat total of fifty seats comprised forty-four constituency seats and six list seats. The respective figures for the remaining parties were as follows: Free Democrats, forty-seven seats of which all were list seats; the Greens, forty-nine seats of which all were list seats; the PDS, thirty seats of which four were constituency seats and twenty-six were list seats.

5.2 Proportionality, parties and politics in Germany

The combination of the bonus seats together with the operation of the 5 per cent electoral threshold has reduced the overall level of proportionality of the German electoral system in recent elections. As Table 5.1 shows, not since the 1950s has Germany experienced such high levels of disproportionality. This reflects the great significance of German unification in 1989. Just as in the late 1940s and 1950s, Germany is passing through a period of electoral instability and change, and this exposes the distortions in the German version of the two-vote system.

There is another interesting trend worth noting in Table 5.1, relating to the 'difference' columns for each of the parties. With few exceptions, the ratio is positive, i.e. the disproportionality of the system usually favours *all* the parties, large and small, with the exceptions of the Free Democrats in 1972 and 1983, and the Greens in 1980, 1983 and 1990. What we are seeing here is the result of the 5 per cent rule. In other words, the system is excluding tiny parties from any representation and all the remaining parties are benefiting from a small surplus in their proportions of seats. It is clear from this table that, despite the distortions of the 5 per cent threshold and the *Überhangmandate* seats, the overall level of disproportionality in German elections is low. For instance, as we shall see, the difference between vote per cent and seat per cent is consistently lower than that produced by the STV in Ireland (see Table 6.2).

It is quite common in debates about electoral reform to draw

Table 5.1   **German federal elections, 1949–94: percentage votes and seats**

	Christian Democratic Union			Christian Social Union			Social Democrats		
	Vote (%)	Seat (%)	Diff. (%)	Vote (%)	Seat (%)	Diff. (%)	Vote (%)	Seat (%)	Diff. (%)
1949	25.2	28.6	+3.4	5.8	6.0	+0.2	29.2	32.6	+3.4
1953	36.4	39.2	+2.8	8.8	10.7	+1.9	28.8	31.0	+2.2
1957	39.7	43.7	+4.0	10.5	10.7	+0.2	31.8	34.0	+2.2
1961	35.8	38.5	+2.7	9.6	10.0	+0.4	36.2	38.1	+1.9
1965	38.0	39.5	+1.5	9.6	9.9	+0.3	39.3	40.7	+1.4
1969	36.6	38.9	+2.3	9.5	9.9	+0.4	42.7	45.2	+2.5
1972	35.2	35.7	+0.5	9.7	9.7	—	45.8	46.4	+0.6
1976	38.0	38.3	+0.3	10.6	10.7	+0.1	42.6	43.1	+0.5
1980	34.2	35.0	+0.8	10.3	10.5	+0.2	42.9	43.9	+1.0
1983	38.2	38.4	+0.2	10.6	10.6	—	38.2	38.8	+0.6
1987	34.5	35.0	+0.5	9.8	9.9	+0.1	37.0	37.4	+0.4
1990	36.7	40.5	+3.8	7.1	7.7	+0.6	33.5	36.1	+2.6
1994	34.2	36.3	+2.1	7.3	7.4	+0.1	36.4	37.5	+1.1

	Free Democrats			Green Party		
	Vote (%)	Seat (%)	Diff. (%)	Vote (%)	Seat (%)	Diff. (%)
1949	11.9	12.9	+1.0			
1953	9.5	9.9	+0.4			
1957	7.7	8.2	+0.5			
1961	12.8	13.4	+0.6			
1965	9.5	9.9	+0.4			
1969	5.8	6.0	+0.2			
1972	8.4	8.3	−0.1			
1976	7.9	7.9	—			
1980	10.6	10.7	+0.1	1.5	0.0	−1.5
1983	7.0	6.8	−0.2	5.6	5.4	−0.2
1987	9.1	9.3	+0.2	8.3	8.5	+0.2
1990	11.0	11.9	+0.9	5.0	1.2	−3.8
1994	6.9	7.0	+0.1	7.3	7.3	—

Note: The vote per cent is the number of 'second', i.e. list, votes. Percentages do not add up to 100 because smaller parties and 'others' have been excluded.
Sources: Mackie and Rose (1991); official returns.

simple conclusions from the experiences of countries using particular systems. For instance, a simplistic analysis of the German party system (before 1990; it becomes a bit more complex after unification) would suggest certain similarities with the British party system. The system comprises two large groupings, one on the Left (Social Democrats) and one on the Right (Christian Democrats), with a small party (the Free Democrats or Liberals) in the centre. There are good and bad points about this pattern. First, it indicates that PR does not have to lead to a proliferation of parties. For most of Germany's post-war history (i.e. since it adopted the two-vote system), it has been a 'two-and-a-half' party system. The early 1980s saw the emergence of the Green Party and in recent years there has also been the emergence of parties representing the 'new Right' (Poguntke with Boll, 1992); these developments have been common to many west European countries (Müller-Rommel, 1989; Müller-Rommel and Pridham, 1991). The basic fact remains, however, that even after all the dis-ruptions associated with unification, the old 'two-and-a-half' parties still remain dominant into the 1990s. To date, Germany's enviable record of strong, stable coalition government remains untouched.

There is a negative side to this issue of the similarity between Germany and the UK – negative at least to those who would not like to see such a system introduced in Britain – and that is the role of the Free Democrats as the 'pivotal' party. As Table 5.2 shows, the Free Democrats have been in almost every post-war German government. The exceptions were in 1957–61, when the Christian Democrats had a sufficiently large number of seats not to need them, and in 1966–69, when the Christian Democrats and Social Democrats formed a 'grand coalition'. There have even been cases in which changes in govern-ment have resulted from a decision of the Free Democrats to switch sides, as happened in 1982 when the Free Democrats switched allegiances from the Social Democrats under Helmut Schmidt, to the Christian Democrats under Helmut Kohl. To some people it is galling to think that a party whose vote share rarely rises to double figures (and whose vote is usually less than that gained by the British Liberals/Liberal Democrats) could have such a hold on the reins of power.

To look at this from another perspective, it can be argued that the Free Democrats serve a useful role in toning down the policies of their more doctrinaire coalition partners. A frequent criticism of the British system is that there can be wide vacillations in policy as power changes hands between the Conservatives and Labour, and that this can be damaging to long-term interests. By contrast, German governments tend to exhibit greater degrees of policy continuity over

Table 5.2   **German federal governments, 1949–94**

Year	Chancellor	Coalition parties
1949	Adenauer	CDU-CSU; FDP; DP
1953	Adenauer	CDU-CSU; FDP (to 1956); DP; GB-BHE (to 1955)
1957	Adenauer	CDU-CSU; DP (to 1960)
1961	Adenauer	CDU-CSU; FDP
1963	Erhard	CDU-CSU; FDP
1965	Erhard	CDU-CSU; FDP
1966	Kiesinger	CDU-CSU; FDP
1969	Brandt	SPD; FDP
1972	Brandt	SPD; FDP
1974	Schmidt	SPD; FDP
1976	Schmidt	SPD; FDP
1980	Schmidt	SPD; FDP
1982	Kohl	CDU-CSU; FDP
1983	Kohl	CDU-CSU; FDP
1987	Kohl	CDU-CSU; FDP
1990	Kohl	CDU-CSU; FDP
1994	Kohl	CDU-CSU; FDP

Note: DP = German Party; GB-BHE = Refugees Party; CDU = Christian Democratic Union; CSU = Christian Social Union; SPD = Social Democratic Party; FDP = Free Democratic Party.
Source: Roberts (1988); official returns.

time – regardless of which parties are in power – to the extent that, in at least some policy domains, it can be suggested that 'parties don't seem to make much of a difference at all' (Gallagher *et al.*, 1995: 344). The Free Democrats can claim some credit for this high degree of policy continuity. (The issue of whether 'pivotal' parties should be seen in a positive or negative light is considered in more detail in chapter 7.)

The two-vote system is frequently extolled in Britain as a panacea to the 'problems' of disproportionality resulting from first past the post. Here, we are told, is a system which incorporates constituency representation while, at the same time, producing proportional election results. This argument presupposes two things: first, that German constituency MPs operate in a similar fashion to British constituency MPs, and second, that the constituency MPs are *seen* as significant within the system. The principal piece of evidence in support of the latter is the fact that the constituency vote is seen as *primary*, as superior to the list vote, indicating that the system attaches more importance to the constituency part of the two-vote election.

However, this is a pretence. As we saw above, what matters in determining the overall allocation of seats is the list vote, not the constituency vote. Furthermore – and this is crucial – there are no by-elections. A retiring or dead politician is replaced by the next highest name on the party list in that region. This applies to both constituency and list replacements, and for one very good reason. If (as, for example, has been proposed in New Zealand, see Mackerras, 1994) list replacements were determined by the next highest name on the list while constituency replacements were decided by by-elections, this would result in a devaluing of constituency seats. A party would not be able to guarantee that it would win the by-election. Therefore, the rational strategy for parties under such a scheme would be to maximize the number of list seats it seeks to win in elections and minimize its constituency seats.

As far as the parties themselves are concerned, therefore, there are no significant differences between the two classes of MPs. This point is reinforced by the parties' campaign strategies, where it is usual for constituency candidates to also have their names on party lists: if they lose one they will almost certainly win the other (providing the party wants them to win and has placed them high enough on the list) (Poguntke, 1994; Roberts, 1975).

The party leaderships may not see the two sets of MPs as different, but evidence from a survey of the members of the Bundestag in the mid-1980s suggests that the constituency MPs do see their role as different from list MPs, paying closer attention to constituency concerns. The bulk of the MPs asked (70 per cent) felt that 'representatives from single-member districts are more accountable' to the voters (Lancaster and Patterson, 1990: 466). This finding may need some qualification, especially when we try to get a true impression of what German MPs mean by constituency service. For instance, it has been stressed by Geoffrey K. Roberts (1975: 221) that the German political culture differs from the British in that German MPs do not have 'a sensitivity toward the constituency relationship; it did not exist before 1949, and has not been highly developed since then'. Furthermore, German voters do not seem very interested in the distinction between the two types of MPs, indeed, '[m]ost voters are completely unaware of the names of their constituency candidates' (Jesse, 1988: 113). Finally, there is the fact that because Germany is a federation, voters have multiple levels of representatives (e.g. *Land* politicians, local councillors) to choose from when raising constituency problems so 'constituency members necessarily play a smaller role in dealing with grievances than in Britain, a unitary and highly centralized country' (Bogdanor, 1984: 57).

There is one important respect in which the two types of seat are quite clearly different: one system disproportionately favours the larger parties. With the recent exception of the PDS (see above), there is little point in smaller parties concentrating their resources on trying to win constituency seats, because, as we have seen, the FPTP electoral system virtually guarantees that they will be unsuccessful. This fact introduces an element of 'strategic voting' into the two-vote system, something which has been exploited with remarkable success by the Free Democrats.

Vote splitting (or split-ticket voting) is a feature of many electoral systems where voters are either voting in different levels of elections at the same time (e.g. the USA or Australia) or where there is a preferential voting system which allows voters to vote across party lines (e.g. Ireland). Germany represents an important example of the latter because the two-vote system, since 1953, allows voters to vote for one party with their first vote and another party with their second. Because smaller parties stand a far better chance in the second-vote, list election, they tend to concentrate their resources on that campaign and, for the most part, treat the first-vote, FPTP election as a lost cause. The Free Democrats have utilized vote splitting to their advantage, encouraging their supporters to vote in a 'coalition fashion' for whichever party they currently share office with. The idea is that Free Democrat supporters should use their constituency votes to support the coalition partner; in return, the coalition partner's supporters are encouraged to give their list vote to the Free Democrats to help it over the 5 per cent hurdle.

Vote splitting has been on the increase: in 1961 just 4.3 per cent of votes were split; by 1987 this figure had increased to 13.7 per cent (Jesse, 1988; Roberts, 1988). Table 5.3 gives an indication of the relationship between vote splitting and party coalition arrangements. Between 1969 and 1982 the Free Democrats were in coalition with the Social Democrats. As the table shows, in all the elections during this period (and particularly in 1972), a large proportion of FDP voters gave their constituency vote to Social Democrat candidates. By contrast, in the 1983 and 1987 elections, when the Free Democrats were in coalition with the Christian Democrats the vote splitting of

Table 5.3   **Constituency votes of FDP list voters, 1961–87 (%)**

Constituency vote to	1961	1965	1969	1972	1976	1980	1983	1987
CDU/CSU	8.1	20.9	10.6	7.9	8.0	13.3	58.3	43.2
SPD	3.1	6.7	24.8	52.9	29.9	35.5	10.1	13.1
FDP	86.5	70.3	62.0	38.2	60.7	48.5	29.1	38.7

Source: Roberts (1988).

the Free Democrats was now predominantly in favour of the Christian Democrats.

5.3 Other two-vote systems

Given the fact that five other countries have recently adopted versions of the two-vote system it is useful to examine some possible variations in how it is or could be used. There are at least four alternatives to the version of the two-vote system used in Germany. First, the electoral formulae in each part can be varied. For instance, in Hungary the constituency seats are determined by the French second ballot system rather than by FPTP. This first distinction is hardly of much significance, since the eventual result is still the same, i.e. it is a proportional result determined by the list vote.

Second, it is possible to alter the proportions of list and con-stituency seats. For instance, in Japan it is proposed that 300 of the 500 parliamentary seats (note the old parliament had 511 seats) will be constituency seats and the remaining 200 seats – distributed across eleven regions – will be elected by PR list (for details, see Shiratori, 1995). In other words, this is a 60 : 40 split compared to the German 50 : 50 split. The Italians, in their recent electoral reforms, have adopted an even more extreme ratio of constituency to list seats: 75 per cent constituency seats and 25 per cent list seats. This raises the question as to what stage the divide becomes so large that the system ceases being proportional? It has been argued that 'at least one-quarter of seats should be adjustment seats, if full reintroduction of PR is desired' (Taagepera and Shugart, 1989: 131). While Italy would appear to just meet that minimal requirement the reality is quite different. It is here where the third possible variation in the two-vote systems occurs.

As was discussed earlier, a core feature of the German electoral system is the notion that list seats should be 'additional' to the constituency seats. To this end, the final seat tally is calculated by subtracting the number of constituency seats each party wins from the total number of list seats to which it is entitled. As Eckhard Jesse (1988: 110) points out, in the mid-1950s there was a debate in Germany about possibly reforming the electoral system. It was proposed that constituency seats should not be *subtracted* from the list seats; rather the two sets of seats should be *added* together. This small technical change in the calculation rules of the two-vote system would have dramatic repercussions for its overall proportionality, a point recognized by the Free Democrats who managed to block it.

The significance of this alteration to the two-vote system (which was dubbed the 'gap' system, or *Grabenwahlsystem*, in Germany) is illustrated by the Italian and Russian cases, both of which use it. The result of the 1994 Italian election (Chamber of Deputies) – the first election held under the new electoral law – is shown in Table 5.4. The final column provides our standard 'difference' trends, i.e. between proportions of votes and seats. Here we see some obvious imbalances produced by the disproportional nature of the electoral system, most notably the right-of-centre, regional *Lega Nord* Party's 10.2 per cent surplus in its seat proportion, and the centrist parties (*Patto per l'Italia*) losing out in their seat proportions by more than 8 per cent.

The table also reveals some unusually proportional results, notably in the case of the parties on the left-of-centre (*Progressisti*), which in most cases appear to have achieved almost perfect parity between their vote and seat proportions. Much of this is due to the operation of the 4 per cent threshold, which in this election 'fell particularly on the left, which won more than half of the "wasted" list votes' (Katz, 1996: 41). It also reflects the fact that the single-member seats generally were contested by alliances, and those alliances negotiated in advance whose candidates would go where, generally on a roughly proportional basis.

The December 1993 Russian election – the first under the new electoral system – produced a multi-party system, with a wide range of parties elected to the parliament, representing a variety of interests (McAllister and White, 1995). Headline news in all media coverage focused on the dramatic electoral victory of the ultra-nationalist

Table 5.4 **The 1994 Italian election: Chamber of Deputies**

	List vote (%)	List seats	Const. seats	Total seats	Total seats (%)	Difference between list votes and total seats (%)
PDS	20.4	37	72	109	17.3	−3.1
Rifondazione Comunista	6.0	12	27	39	6.2	+0.2
PSI	2.2	0	14	14	2.2	—
Verdi	2.7	0	11	11	1.7	−1.0
Rete	1.9	0	6	6	1.0	−0.9
Alleanza Democratica	1.2	0	18	18	2.9	+1.7
Cristiano-Sociali	—	—	5	5	0.8	n.a.
Rinascita Socialista	—	—	1	1	0.2	n.a.
Independent Left	—	—	10	10	1.6	n.a.
Total Progressisti	*34.3*	*49*	*164*	*213*	*33.8*	*n.a.*
PPI	11.1	29	4	33	5.2	−5.9
Patto Segni	4.7	13	0	13	2.1	−2.6
Total Patto per l'Italia	*15.7*	*42*	*4*	*46*	*7.3*	*−8.4*
Forza Italia	21.0	32	108	140	22.2	+1.2
Alleanza Nazionale	13.5	22	87	109	17.3	+3.8
Lega Nord	8.4	10	107	117	18.6	+10.2
Lista Pannella	3.5	0	0	0	0	−3.5
Total Poli	*46.4*	*64*	*302*	*366*	*58.1*	*+11.7*
Total Other	*3.6*	*0*	*5*	*5*	*0.8*	*−2.8*
Total	**100.0**	**155**	**475**	**630**	**100.0**	

Notes: To minimize details, this table treats the parties involved in the alliance with Forza Italia as one party. The parties in question are: Polo della Libertà, Polo del Buon Governo, CCD, UDC, Polo Liberal-Democratico and Riformatori. This ignores the fact that the nature of the 'alliance' varied wildly in different parts of the country and that, after the election, some of these parties formed separate parliamentary groups.
Source: Adapted from Katz (1996).

Liberal Democratic Party of Russia (LDPR) led by the outspoken Vladimir Zhirinovsky. With almost a quarter (23 per cent) of the total vote, the LDPR won more votes than any other party. As a result Zhirinovsky and his party were propelled into the limelight as representing a clear threat to the leadership of President Boris Yeltsin, whose preferred party, the reformist Russia's Choice, had been beaten into second place (15 per cent).

What seems to have escaped the attention of many of the observers is the fact that even though the LDPR won by far the most votes in the system, it did not win the most seats. It ended up with seventy seats (16 per cent) as compared with ninety-six seats (22 per cent) for Russia's Choice. As Table 5.5 shows, the discrepancy was due to the large number of constituency seats won by Russia's Choice (fifty-six seats, as against just eleven seats for the LDPR). Had the Russians been using the German version of the two-vote system, the election result would have been very different. Instead of adding the list and constituency totals together, the result would be based on subtracting one from the other. The final result for the LDPR would have probably been of the order of a hundred seats, while Russia's Choice would have had ended up with less than seventy seats. It is in the discrepancy between votes won and seats awarded for the two biggest parties that we see the highest scores in the difference column of Table 5.5: Russia's Choice benefited by 6.2 per cent in its proportion of seats, while the LDPR was 7 per cent down on the proportion of seats it should have won if the system had been properly proportional.

The 1995 parliamentary elections revealed some further quirks in the Russian version of the two-vote system (see Table 5.6). In comparison with 1993, when thirteen parties fielded candidates, in the 1995 election forty-three parties succeeded in registering for election (gathering the required 200,000 signatures). The number of candidates leaped to 5,675, three times more than in 1993. In some constituencies there were as many as twenty-five candidates, so that in some cases the ballot paper was the size of a broadsheet newspaper page (Belin, 1996: 15). The effect of such a large number of parties was to produce a highly disproportional result. Only four parties (LDPR, Communist Party, Yabloko and Our Home is Russia) managed to cross the 5 per cent threshold required to win list seats. (For ease of comparison, the parties have been listed in the same order as in Table 5.5.) Between them, these four parties amassed 50.5 per cent of the vote: almost half of the voters supported parties that failed to win party list seats, causing the leaders of Yabloko to note, with some glee, how the electoral system succeeded in ensuring that 'microscopic intriguers with gigantic ambitions were eliminated' (cited in Orttung, 1996: 6). As Robert Orttung (1996: 7) observes: 'The 5 per

Table 5.5 **The 1993 Russian election: state duma**

	List vote (%)	List seats	Const. seats	Total seats	Total seats (%)	Difference between list votes and total seats (%)
Russia's Choice	15.4	40	56	96	21.6	+6.2
LDPR	22.8	59	11	70	15.8	−7.0
Communist Party	12.4	32	33	65	14.6	+2.2
Agrarian Party	7.9	21	26	47	10.6	+2.7
Women of Russia	8.1	21	4	25	5.6	−2.5
Yabloko	7.8	20	13	33	7.4	−0.4
Party of Russian Unity and Accord	6.8	18	9	27	6.1	−0.7
Democratic Party of Russia	5.5	14	7	21	4.7	−0.8
Others	13.3	0	60*	60	13.5	n.a.
Total	100.0	225	219**	444	99.9	

Notes: * 'Others' included the following: Civic Union for Stablization; Justice and Progress 18; Movement for Democratic Reforms 8; Dignity and Mercy 3; Future of Russia 1; Independents 30.
** Six seats in the State Duma were left vacant after a boycott of the election in Chechnya, and postponents of the election in Tatarstan and Chelyabinsk.
Source: Keesing's Record of World Events.

cent barrier greatly benefited the four parties that managed to cross it, essentially doubling the value of every vote they won.'

Once again the constituency seats served to increase the vote–seat distortions in the Russian electoral system. The biggest beneficiary from this was the Communist Party which won fifty-eight constituency seats, increasing its already inflated seat total to 34.9 per cent and awarding it with a 12.6 per cent surplus in its share of total parliamentary seats (when compared with its vote). Once again the LDPR lost out on its constituency seats, this time only managing to win one, leading one commentator to suggest that this revealed 'that the organization itself has little depth beyond its leader' (Orttung, 1996: 8). However, LDPR's weakness in the constituencies was, in part, compensated for by the inflation in its list seats caused by the exclusion of the smaller parties (for not passing the 5 per cent threshold), and as a result – unlike the 1993 election – the LDPR total

Table 5.6 **The 1995 Russian election: state duma**

	List vote (%)	List seats	Const. seats	Total seats	Total seats (%)	Difference between list votes and total seats (%)
Russia's Democratic Choice	4.0	0	9	9	2.0	−2.0
LDPR	11.2	50	1	51	11.3	+0.1
Communist Party	22.3	99	58	157	34.9	+12.6
Agrarian Party	3.9	0	20	20	4.4	−0.5
Women of Russia	4.6	0	3	3	0.7	−3.9
Yabloko	6.9	31	14	45	10.0	+3.1
Our Home is Russia	10.1	45	10	55	12.2	+2.1
Power to the People	n.a.	0	9	9	2.0	n.a.
Congress of Russian Communities	4.3	0	5	5	1.1	−3.2
Party of Workers' Self-Management	4.0	0	0	0	0.0	−4.0
Communists/Working Russia	4.6	0	0	0	0.0	−4.6
Others*	24.1	0	95	95	21.1	n.a.
Total	100.0	225	225	450	99.7	

Notes: * Independent candidates won 77 of the 225 single-member seats while a number of small parties won up to three seats each.
Source: Keesing's Record of World Events.

share of parliamentary seats (11.3 per cent) matched its vote share (11.2 per cent).

Given what we have seen of the Italian and Russian cases, the question needs to be raised whether in fact it is appropriate to include these electoral systems in the general two-vote category. In each case we have seen quite large discrepancies between vote and seat shares, in some instances as high as 10 per cent or more. At best, these systems can be seen as only 'contingently proportional' (Dunleavy and Margetts, 1995: 12). And, particularly in the case of the Italian system where just 25 per cent of the seats are list seats, it is probably more appropriate to categorize it as a variant of FPTP.

One final alternative to the current German two-vote system is to remove the 'two-vote' element altogether while retaining the basic distinction between the two types of MP. As we saw above, such a system was initially used in the Federal Republic of Germany between 1949–53, when voters voted just once and their vote was used twice: (1) to elect the constituency candidate, and (2) to add to the party total in the regional list. As was pointed out in the previous chapter (p. 80), the Italian Senate has adopted such a system. The effect of removing the two-vote element is to turn this system into a version of two-tier districting, which as we saw in chapter 4 (pp. 69–70) is quite common in list systems.

This hybrid system (referred to colloquially as 'the German system') was proposed for Britain in 1976 by the Hansard Society. As we saw in chapter 2, in the light of electoral developments in Britain in the first part of the 1970s, the Hansard Society established an independent Commission, chaired by Lord Blake, to examine poss- ible alternatives to FPTP. The Commission's report, issued in June 1976, proposed that the House of Commons' membership should be reduced to 640 members, three-quarters of whom would be elected for single-seat constituencies by FPTP, while one-quarter would be allocated seats on the basis of the 'best losers' among defeated candidates in different regions of the country.

There were two main reasons for these proposed changes to the two-vote system. First, there was a desire to avoid any potential confusion by introducing a new, more complicated system. In other words, the issue of 'simplicity' was once against foremost in the minds of British electoral reformers. The system proposed by the Hansard Society required no change to voting procedures; the British voter would simply mark an 'X' next to his or her preferred candidate. The second concern of the Hansard Society was to avoid the German practice of allowing candidates two attempts to get elected. As we saw above, it is common for German constituency candidates to also have a place on party lists as a guarantee against possible defeat in the first vote. The view of Blake's Commission was that this practice should be avoided.

Clearly there were a number of features to the Hansard Society's proposals which were seen as attractive to a British audience. The system would be simple; it would avoid the need for party lists, and all candidates would have to compete for constituency seats. How- ever, the fundamental question is would it actually be a proportional system? The 25 per cent of 'top-up' seats would not be determined on a proportional basis; rather, they would be made up of the 'best losers' in each region. Such a system would be prone to all sorts of

distortions (see Bogdanor, 1984: 71–3). Parties with high concentrations of geographical support would benefit disproportionately. Best
losers in constituencies with small numbers of candidates would stand
a far better chance than best losers in constituencies with more
candidates. Furthermore, the proposal to also include a 5 per cent
threshold would have resulted in small parties fielding a greater
number of candidates to boost their overall vote in a region. Arguably
one consequence of this would be that more MPs would be elected on
a minority vote than is currently the case in Britain. In short, there are
a number of reasons for arguing that, if anything, the Hansard
Society's proposals would have actually *increased* the levels of
disproportionality in British elections. The degree to which such a
proposal could be categorized as belonging to the 'family' of two-
vote systems is highly debatable.

5.4 Testing the two-vote system on British voters

As part of their study of the application of different electoral systems
to the British case, Dunleavy and his colleagues tested the two-vote
system (referred to by them as the additional member system) on their
sample of British voters. Table 5.7 reproduces the result of their
simulated election, broken down by region, and showing comparisons
with the actual 1992 general election results (under FPTP). As in the
case of the simulation in chapter 3 (and in chapter 6), the most
significant difference between the two-vote and FPTP results is that
there would have been a 'hung parliament'. Both large parties would
have been awarded fewer seats (the Conservatives would have sixty-
eight fewer seats, Labour thirty-nine). The biggest gains would have
been by the Liberal Democrats whose seat tally would have risen
to 116.

Disguised by the features in this highly proportional result is the
reality that most of the smaller parties' gains would have been in list
seats: the Liberal Democrats would have just six constituency seats;
the nationalist parties just two. To test the significance of this,
Dunleavy *et al.* gave their respondents a mock two-vote ballot (much
like the German version reproduced in Figure 5.1), thus allowing
voters an opportunity to split their vote between two parties if they so
wished. As we saw above, the German experience has been for
supporters of the smaller Free Democrat Party (FDP) to give their list

Table 5.7   Parties' seats in Britain under the two-vote system compared with the 1992 FPTP election result: the Rowntree/ICM survey

	No. of seats	Con.	Lab.	Lib./Dem.	SNP/PC
South	261	131	72	58	0
North and Midlands	263	107	114	42	0
Scotland	72	19	27	11	15
Wales	38	11	19	5	3
Britain	634	268	232	116	18
Actual result in 1992	634	336	271	20	7
Net change in seats		−68	−39	+96	+11

Source: Derived from Dunleavy *et al.* (1992: Table 6).

votes to the FDP, but, on balance, to give their constituency votes to the party's proposed coalition partner (lately the Christian Democrats). This 'vote splitting' is a rational response by small-party supporters to the exigencies of the two-vote system. Rather surprisingly, in this experiment the UK voters tend to be quite different. Those British respondents with Liberal Democrat leanings were more inclined to support the Liberal Democrats at the *constituency* stage than at the *list* stage. Dunleavy *et al.* comment (1992: 8) that 'the two-vote . . . approach seems only to encourage people to ''waste'' their votes', and so they suggest that the Hansard Society's proposal for a single-vote version of this system would make more sense in the UK context. Arguably this conclusion is somewhat premature as it makes no allowance for the possibility that the respondents might not have understood the full implications of the two-vote system; nor does it allow for the possible appeal of prominent Liberal Democratic candidates, accustomed to treating general elections as a series of individual by-elections. Under a real two-vote election the party would presumably adopt a very different electoral strategy.

5.5   Conclusion

As was pointed out in the introduction to this book, the field of electoral research has long been stagnant and unchanging, reflecting the fact that few countries were prepared to countenance electoral change. Events in recent years have dramatically changed that picture, not only because of the process of democratization on the European continent, but also because of recent electoral reforms in three long-established democracies: Italy, Japan and New Zealand. What is most telling about two of these cases, Japan and New Zealand, is that they have opted for a version of the two-vote system, and they have been joined in this move by Hungary.

As we saw above, Italy (in the Chamber of Deputies) and Russia have also adopted new electoral systems which, prima facie, share certain features of the two-vote system. However, the fact that in both of these cases (and, indeed, in Japan) the list seats do not compensate for the distorting effects of the first past the post constituency elections (which in the Italian case accounts for 75 per cent of total seats), precludes us from including these cases under the two-vote category.

The two-vote system appears to be in fashion at present. The successful model of post-war (West) German politics is held up as testimony to its achievements. However, now that the system is being used in other places, there will be an ideal opportunity to test once and for all whether this system has all the attributes that German experience has for so long suggested. Giovanni Sartori (1994: 75) is doubtful. Referring to this system as a 'plurality-PR hybrid', he suggests that it 'advocates ... belief that they are bringing together the best of two worlds; but they are likely to obtain, instead a bastard-producing hybrid which combines [the] defects' of PR and FPTP.

Notes

[1] As we saw in the previous chapter, the new electoral system for the Italian Senate also shares in common this aspect of the voter having only one vote. For this reason, this system does not fit into the two-vote category and so will not be included in this chapter.

[2] This system is referred to in Germany as the 'Niemeyer method'. Prior to 1985 the list seats were determined by the highest average system using d'Hondt divisors. In other words, Germany adopted more proportional counting rules in 1985, making it easier for small parties to win seats.

[3] In fact a number of the *Land* electoral systems compensate for *Überhang-mandate* seats, so that the other parties are also granted extra seats (Nohlen, 1989: 231–3). No such compensation applies for Bundestag elections.

6
THE SINGLE TRANSFERABLE VOTE SYSTEM OF PROPORTIONAL REPRESENTATION

The origins of the single transferable vote (STV) system of proportional representation (PR) date back to the mid-nineteenth century. The two people credited most with its 'invention' – operating independently, and apparently without knowledge, of each other – are Thomas Hare (1806–92; an English lawyer) and Carl George Andrae (1812–93; a Danish mathematician and politician).[1] Of the two, it was Hare who played the larger role. As we saw in chapter 2, Hare's *Treatise on the Election of Representatives, Parliamentary and Municipal* (1859) – and its subsequent amended editions – provided a considerable impetus to the debate about suffrage extension and the electoral system in Britain. Key figures, among them the philosopher, John Stuart Mill, enthusiastically endorsed Hare's proposals (Hart, 1992).

From the very beginning, STV has had its supporters. Indeed, if one were to carry out a head count of the scholars writing about electoral systems today, it is likely that many would rate STV very highly. On the face of it, there appear to be good reasons for this, for here is a system which is both proportional *and* which facilitates constituency politicians. In contrast to the list systems of PR, under the STV system the electors vote for candidates, not parties; electors stand a better chance of seeing their preferred candidate elected; and, unlike first past the post (FPTP) and the majoritarian systems, the voters have a choice between a number of constituency politicians.

STV appears attractive, and yet one is left with the nagging question: why is it so infrequently used? Why is it that after a process of democratization in Spain, Portugal and Greece in the late 1970s and after an even more dramatic process of democratization across eastern and central Europe and the former Soviet Union in the late 1980s, with just the one small and temporary exception of Estonia from 1989–92 (Taagepera, 1990; Wilder, 1993), STV was not the chosen electoral system? Why is it that, after a long period when few established democracies changed their electoral systems (France being possibly the sole exception), that once a flurry of change does occur – in Italy, Japan and New Zealand – again STV is passed over? If STV is apparently so popular among the scholars, why is it avoided by the politicians?

There is a particular British perspective to this question. As we saw in chapter 2, throughout this century STV has featured repeatedly as the preferred system of pressure groups clamouring for reform of the British electoral system. It was very nearly adopted in the UK as a result of the 1917 Speaker's Conference. Ultimately it was used for some political elections in the UK: between 1918–50 for four of the seven university seats; in the 1920s and again since 1973 for all elections other than Westminster elections in Northern Ireland. It is the preferred system of the Liberal Democrats and is actively promoted by the British Electoral Reform Society. It is used by a plethora of societies and organizations for their elections. In addition, it has also been noted by Vernon Bogdanor that: 'Apart from a brief experiment in Denmark in the 1850s, STV has been used only in countries which have at some time been under British rule.' And, he adds: 'It is the "Anglo-Saxon" method of securing proportional representation' (Bogdanor, 1984: 76). Arend Lijphart (1987:100) goes so far as to suggest that 'we still have a perfect social science law without any major exceptions – very rare in the social sciences – linking political culture with forms of PR. When Anglo-American countries use PR, they always choose STV; in other countries, the choice is list PR'. With the exception of New Zealand (the first Anglo-Saxon country to adopt a form of list PR in 1993) and also the temporary exception of Estonia (which is not Anglo-Saxon), this point still applies. STV is currently used by the following countries for their national elections: Australia (for elections to the Senate, the upper house), the Republic of Ireland (for all elections other than presidential elections) and Malta (for elections to the unicameral parliament). It is used at a regional level in several states in Australia (most notably in Tasmania; also by four other states); it is used for local and European Parliament elections in Northern Ireland, and it is used for certain local elections in several states in the USA.

These cases all share one thing in common – their small size. Only Australia, with a population of just over sixteen million, can lay claim to being a moderately large system. As we shall see below, in part to facilitate the use of STV in a larger system, Australia has adopted a particular variant of STV for its Senate elections. The fact is, however, that Australia's population is far smaller than Britain's, and, in any event, Australia does not use STV for its more important lower house elections. The only two countries which do – the Irish Republic (with a three-and-a-half million population) and Malta (with just 343,000) – are arguably far too small to provide adequate examples of what a larger country might expect if it switched to STV. This is one of the main problems for STV proponents to contend with; it also partially answers the question raised above about why STV is not popular among the politicians – because they see it as Utopian, as suitable only for smaller countries where constituencies do not have to be too large.

There are, of course, other reasons why politicians have tended to reject STV. Some of these were raised in the recent report of the British Labour Party's Plant Working Party (Labour Party, 1993). These are assessed later in the chapter. Given the fact that much of this chapter focuses on the Irish case, we start, in section 6.1, with a brief account of how Ireland ended up using STV. Section 6.2 deals with the operation of STV and is followed, in section 6.3, with a discussion of its principal characteristics: what distinguishes it from the other electoral systems; its positive and negative features. The chapter ends, in section 6.4, with an assessment of whether STV is appropriate for larger countries such as the UK.

6.1 STV in Ireland

We saw in chapter 2 how in the first part of this century, the proponents of PR had a tough – and ultimately unsuccessful – battle in trying to effect electoral reform in Britain. Ireland, however, presented a special case. From the moment that Home Rule appeared on the horizon, repeated references were made in the parliamentary debates to the need for some form of 'protection' for the 'loyal Irish minority' (Hart, 1992: 104, *passim*). There was some sympathy, therefore, for the idea that PR – specifically STV – might be introduced in Ireland (and, for that matter, also in Scotland, Malta and parts of India – Hart, 1992: 200). With the growing likelihood of Home Rule, and the belief that this would result in some form of partition of the island, there was a desire to placate the fears of southern Irish Unionists. In 1911, the president of the PR Society, Lord Courtney, was invited to Dublin to give a public lecture on STV. This resulted in the formation of the PR Society of Ireland in the same year, including in its membership Arthur Griffith, the founder of the secessionist party, Sinn Féin. He was on record for his praise of PR as ensuring 'that minorities shall be represented in proportion to their strength. It is the one just system of election under democratic government' (cited in O'Leary, 1979: 6).

As Cornelius O'Leary (1979) observes, the original Irish Home Rule Bill of 1912 did not contain any provisions for PR, but in the ensuing debates, amendments were carried proposing the adoption of STV for a proportion of the seats in the proposed Irish House of Commons. The outbreak of the First World War caused the deferment of further debate (and any enactment) of Home Rule in Ireland for the time being. It was not until 1918 that STV appeared once more on the agenda, as a result of a private member's bill by an Irish Nationalist MP, Thomas Scanlon. He proposed the adoption of STV for municipal elections in his west of Ireland constituency of Sligo, arguing that this would encourage the Protestant minority to play a more active role in local politics. His bill was passed, and in December 1918 the first STV election for any part of the UK was held in Sligo, producing an impressive result for the Protestant minority. This result, as O'Leary (1979: 8) points out, was 'hailed as a triumph'. The (then) pro-Unionist *Irish Times* referred to STV as 'the *magna charta* of political and municipal minorities' (quoted in Proportional Representation Society, 1919). The local *Sligo Champion* was gushing in its praise: 'The system has justified its adoption. We saw it work; we saw its simplicity; we saw its unerring honesty to the voter all through; and we saw the result in the final count; and we join in the

general expression of those who followed it through with an in-
telligent interest – it is as easy as the old way; it is a big improvement
and it is absolutely fair' (ibid.).

In the light of this result and its contrast with the dramatic electoral
gains across all of southern Ireland by Sinn Féin in the 1918 general
election (held under FPTP), the Lloyd George government passed an
act proposing STV for all local authorities in Ireland with the
intention of trying to limit some of Sinn Féin's electoral gains.
Subsequently, in 1920, the first set of all-Ireland local elections with
STV were held. Sinn Féin still managed to make dramatic gains in
southern Ireland, but in northern Ireland the use of STV prevented
Sinn Féin from gaining overall control of a number of councils.

Lloyd George's 1920 Government of Ireland Act (which ultimately was only ever enacted in northern Ireland) contained a clause
proposing STV for both parts of the partitioned island. (In the mid-
1920s the new Northern Ireland administration replaced STV with
FPTP and this remained in operation until the 1970s.) The subsequent
Anglo-Irish Treaty of 1921, establishing the Irish Free State in the
twenty-six counties of southern Ireland, did not contain any explicit
conditions relating to the electoral system for the new state; however,
there was a notion that the rights of the minority Protestant community should somehow be protected. To an extent this would be
achieved via the membership of the upper chamber of the new Irish
parliament. It would also be achieved by the adoption of a PR system.
O'Leary (1979: 14) suggests two other reasons why STV was
adopted in the first Irish constitution of 1922: first, it followed a
pattern in all new emergent states around that time, where PR was
being adopted without debate, and second, the work of the PR Society
(including the Irish branch) ensured that PR was high on the
agenda.

A curious feature of the Irish case is that, to an extent, it could be
argued that the particular form of PR – namely STV – which was
introduced may have had more to do with ignorance of other systems,
than to a preference for one form of PR over another. The basic point
of interest is that the 1922 constitution merely stated that the electoral
system shall be 'PR'. It was not until the new constitution of 1937
that there was an explicit reference to 'STV' as the particular form of
PR to be used in Ireland. In his detailed examination of the debates
surrounding the adoption of the 1922 constitution, O'Leary (1979:
15) points out that there was little discussion of the particularities of

the proposed electoral system and, if anything, '[t]he speeches revealed a complete ignorance of the List systems'.

Having been introduced into Ireland almost by accident, STV's retention as Ireland's electoral system has since been debated on two occasions in some detail and the decision to retain it has been quite deliberate. The current constitution of 1937 states that Ireland's electoral system is STV. To change this provision requires a referendum. In 1959 and again in 1968 there were attempts by the Fianna Fáil party to replace STV with FPTP. The motivation on each occasion was to increase the party's chances of forming a single-party, majority government for, despite the fact that by 1958 Fianna Fáil had been in power for twenty-one of the previous twenty-seven years, it had only enjoyed an overall majority on four occasions. The party's founder, Eamonn de Valera, was due to retire soon and there was a fear that without him the party's chances of ever achieving an overall majority of seats would be greatly reduced. A referendum on electoral reform was called to coincide with the 1959 presidential election, in which de Valera, retiring as prime minister, was the Fianna Fáil candidate. This was seen as a cynical move designed to ensure the easy passage of the referendum bill. In the event, the bill was narrowly defeated (despite de Valera's easy victory), with 48 per cent voting in favour, 52 per cent against. The fact that Fianna Fáil's proposal was defeated by such a small margin (just 33,667 votes) encouraged the party to have another go, just nine years later, in 1968 (Sinnott, 1993: 76). This time the proposal was resoundingly defeated, with 39 per cent voting in favour of replacing STV, 61 per cent voting against.

6.2 How STV works

STV differs from the other systems we have dealt with so far in terms of all three features of electoral systems, i.e. district magnitude, ballot structure and electoral formula. Being a proportional system, STV operates with a district magnitude greater than one (thus distinguishing it from FPTP and the majoritarian systems discussed in chapters 2 and 3). In other words, more than one MP is elected per constituency, e.g. in Ireland the range is between three and five MPs; in some parts of Australia there can be more than twenty MPs in a constituency. Hare had proposed that the whole of the UK should be one vast constituency; that electors should be able to choose between all candidates for the House of Commons. This proposal was never adopted as electoral engineers realized that it would be hopelessly unrealistic to expect voters to choose between thousands of different candidates. As we shall see below, the fact that, for the most part, STV tends to operate with relatively small constituencies has important implications for the question of proportionality.

Another area of variation between STV and other electoral systems is over the ballot structure which is ordinal. Ordinal voting refers to the right of electors to vote for as many, or as few, candidates on the ballot paper as they wish; they can vote across party lines. Voters are advised to declare as many preferences as possible, so as to maximize the influence of their vote in the final election result. In Ireland electors need only mark one preference if they wish. In Australian elections, in order to have a valid vote, electors must vote a set minimum number of preferences. The precise number varies in different parts of Australia (e.g. in Senate elections they must vote for all candidates).

Figure 6.1 provides an example of a recent Irish ballot paper for the Dublin North-Central constituency (four seats to be filled). Note how each of the large parties (Fianna Fáil and Fine Gael) have more than one candidate and how the candidates are listed alphabetically. Ballot papers vary considerably across the different STV systems: all the other STV systems list the candidates under their different party groupings, as shown in Figure 6.2 which is an example of a recent ballot paper for a general election in Malta.

STV also differs from other electoral systems with regard to electoral formula. Because STV operates in multi-member constituencies, some method is required to determine which candidates are elected and which are not. A quota – known as the 'Droop quota', named after its nineteenth-century inventor, the mathematician and lawyer, H. R. Droop – is calculated which ensures that exactly the correct number of candidates are elected in each constituency. Ordinarily, to be elected, a candidate must have as least as many votes as set by the quota. The quota is calculated as follows:

$$\text{`Droop quota'} = \left[\frac{\text{total valid votes}}{\text{(total number of seats)} + 1} \right] + 1$$

The easiest way to understand how the Droop quota works is to

Marcáil ord do rogha sna spáis seo síos. Mark order of preference in spaces below.	Marc Oifigiúl Official Mark ➤
	BARLOW-COMMUNITY (Hannah Barlow-Community, of 67, Shantalla, Beaumont, Dublin. Alderman, Housewife, Midwife.)
	BELTON—FINE GAEL (Paddy Belton, of Ballivor, Howth, Co. Dublin. Director of Family Business.)
	BIRMINGHAM—FINE GAEL (George Birmingham, of "Denville", 498 Howth Road, Raheny, Dublin 5. City Councillor and Barrister-at-Law.)
	BRADY—FIANNA FÁIL (Vincent Brady, of 138, Kincora Road, Dublin 3. Company Director.)
	BROWNE—SOCIALIST LABOUR PARTY (Noel Browne, of Stepaside, Church Road, Malahide, Dublin. Medical Doctor)
	BYRNE—FINE GAEL (Mary Byrne, of 177, Seafield Road, Clontarf, Dublin 3 City Councillor.)
	CURLEY—THE COMMUNIST PARTY OF IRELAND (John Curley, of 44, Greencastle Road, Coolock, Dublin 5. Storeman.)
	DILLON (Andrew Dillon, of Drumnigh, Portmarnock, Co. Dublin. Solicitor.)
	DOHERTY (Vincent Doherty, of 76, Pembroke Road, Dublin. H Blocks Campaigner.)
	HAUGHEY—FIANNA FÁIL (Charles J. Haughey, of Abbeville, Kinsealy, Malahide, Co. Dublin. Taoiseach.)
	MARTIN—THE LABOUR PARTY (Michael Martin, of 28, Seafield Road. Insurance Agent.)
	O'HALLORAN—THE LABOUR PARTY (Michael O'Halloran, of 141, Ardlea Road, Artane. Public Representative and Trade Union Official.)
	TIMMONS—FIANNA FÁIL (Eugene Timmons, of 42, Copeland Avenue, Dublin 3. Public Representative.)

TREORACHA

I. Féach chuige go bhfuil an marc oifigiúil ar an bpáipéar.

II. Scríobh an figiúr 1 le hais ainm an chéad iarrthóra is rogha leat, an figiúr 2 le hais do dhara rogha agus mar sin de.

III. Fill an páipéar ionas nach bhfeicfear do vóta. Taispeáin *cúl an pháipéir* don oifigeach ceannais, agus cuir sa bhosca ballóide é.

INSTRUCTIONS

I. See that the official mark is on the paper.

II. Write 1 beside the name of the candidate of your first choice, 2 beside your second choice, and so on.

III. Fold the paper to conceal your vote. Show *the back of the paper* to the presiding officer and put it in the ballot box.

Figure 6.1   Irish single transferable vote ballot paper

No. of Members to be elected .... Division		
Mark order of preference	**Badge of Candidate**	**Names of Candidates**
		PARTIT TAL-FJURI
	🌼	JONES, (John Jones, of 52 Old Bakery Street, Valletta, Merchant)
	🌼	MAGRO, (William David Magro, of 10 Tower Road, Sliema (Painter)
	🌼	MIFSUD, (Joseph Mifsud, of 16 Victoria Avenue, Sliema, Labourer)
	🌼	MUSCAT, (Francesco Muscat of 1 St. Paul's Str. Zabbar Driver)
	🌼	VELLA, (James Vella, of 5 Republic Street, St. Julians Architect
	🌼	WILLIAMS, (Francis Williams of 85 Genuis Street, Zurrieq Chemist)
		PARTIT TAL- GHASFUR
	🦅	AZZOPARDI, (Spiro Azzopardi, of 13 Marina Street, Zejtun, Printer)
	🦅	BORG, (Assuero Borg, of 69 Barbara Street, Mellieha, Clerk)
	🦅	CASSAR, (Lela Cassar, of "Dolores", Main Street, Cospiuca, Housewife)
	🦅	MIZZI, (Glormu Mizzi, of 70 Two Gates Str. Lija, Lawyer)
	🦅	ZARB, (Fortunat Zarb, of 15 Strait Street, Luqa, Clerk)
		PARTIT TAS-SIĠAR
	🌳	AZZOPARDI, (Reginald Azzopardi, of 165 St. Domenic Str., Qormi, Clerk)
	🌳	ZAMMIT, (Lawrence Zammit of "Josdor", 188 Bwieraq Str. Hamrun, Chemist)
		KANDIDATI INDIPENDENTI
		BUHAGIAR, (Louis Buhagiar, of 55 Republic Street, Zabbar, Merchant)
		GALEA, (Ninu Galea, of 67 B'Kara Lane, Qrendi, Worker)

Figure 6.2 **Malta single transferable vote ballot paper**

imagine a scenario where the total number of valid votes is 100. As we know, STV works with multi-seat constituencies; this is the principal characteristic distinguishing STV from the majoritarian systems dealt with in chapter 3. In fact, the Droop quota can be easily applied to the alternative vote system used for Australian lower house elections. Since the alternative vote operates with single-seat constituencies (and hence is not proportional), the Droop quota is as follows: $(100/1+1)+1 = 51$ votes. In other words, to be elected under the alternative vote system, a candidate needs at least fifty-one votes or 51 per cent of the total vote, a majoritarian result. When there is more than one seat to be filled in a constituency, the minimum number of votes required to be elected is reduced. In a three-seat constituency a candidate requires 26 per cent of the vote; in a four-seat constituency, 21 per cent; in a five-seat constituency, 17 per cent. The greater the number of seats to be filled, i.e. the larger the district magnitude, the lower the number of votes required to be elected. This fact has important implications for the issue of proportionality, as we shall see below.

Table 6.1 shows an example of an election count using STV. The Donegal South-West constituency in the 1992 election was a three-seat constituency. Nine candidates were fielded: two each by Fianna Fáil, Fine Gael and Sinn Féin; one by Democratic Left; and two independent candidates. The total number of valid votes (after subtracting the invalid votes) was 29,808, producing a quota of 7,453 votes.

The first count in an STV election involves the sorting of all the ballot papers according to the first preferences of the voters. If we were using a version of the FPTP system in multi-seat constituencies (i.e. the limited vote as used in Britain in the 1870s, see chapter 2), the first three candidates with the greatest number of votes from the following list would be elected, with Fine Gael's Jimmy White just pipping his running mate, Dinny McGinley, by 241 votes:

	Vote	Distance from quota
1 Pat the Cope Gallagher (Fianna Fáil)	7,870	+ 417
2 Mary Coughlan (Fianna Fáil)	6,639	− 814
3 Jim White (Fine Gael)	5,745	−1,708
4 Dinny McGinley (Fine Gael)	5,504	−1,949

However, since the electoral system being used here is STV, only those candidates with at least as many votes as the electoral quota are

Table 6.1   Counting an STV election: the Donegal South-West constituency in 1992

Names of candidates	First count Number of votes	Second count Transfer of Gallagher's surplus and result	Third count Transfer of McCluskey's votes and result	Fourth count Transfer of Coll's votes and result	Fifth count Transfer of Mooney's votes and result	Sixth count Transfer of Doherty's votes and result	Seventh count Transfer of Rodger's votes and result
Coll, Fred	539	+12 / 551	+6 / 557	−557 / —			—
*Coughlan, Mary (F. F.)	6,639	+276 / 6,915	+47 / 6,962	+71 / 7,033	+145 / 7,178	+139 / 7,317	+307 / 7,624
Doherty, Anna Rose (S. F.)	577	+6 / 583	+245 / 828	+27 / 855	+50 / 905	−905 / —	—
*Gallagher, Pat the Cope (F. F.)	7,870	−417 / 7,453	7,453	7,453	7,453	7,453	7,453
McCluskey, John (S. F.)	409	+3 / 412	−412 / —				
*McGinley, Dinny (F. G.)	5,504	+60 / 5,564	+12 / 5,576	+155 / 5,731	+124 / 5,855	+82 / 5,937	+651 / 6,588
Mooney, Benny	700	+5 / 705	+6 / 711	+54 / 765	−765 / —		—
Rodgers, Séamus (D. L.)	1,825	+38 / 1,863	+18 / 1,881	+93 / 1,974	+84 / 2,058	+143 / 2,201	−2,201 / —
White, Jim (F. G.)	5,745	+17 / 5,762	+30 / 5,792	+44 / 5,836	+130 / 5,966	+43 / 6,009	+370 / 6,379
Non-transferable papers	—	—	+48 / 48	+113 / 161	+232 / 393	+498 / 891	+873 / 1,764
Total	29,808	29,808	29,808	29,808	29,808	29,808	29,808

Total vote: 30,496

Total valid vote: 29,808

Number of seats: 3

Quota: 7,453

Candidates elected:
Gallagher
Coughlan
McGinley

Note: * Sitting MPs.
Source: Election returns.

deemed elected. In this case just one candidate, Pat the Cope Gallagher, met this requirement, and he was duly elected. Two seats were left to be filled, requiring a second count. The next count, under STV, involves one of two things. If a candidate is elected, the next count usually consists of the transfer of all surplus votes, i.e. of the number of votes by which he or she has exceeded the quota. If no candidate has been elected (or if the surplus is too small to make any difference to the candidates left in the race), the next count entails the 'elimination' of the candidate with the least votes and the transfer of his or her votes to the remaining candidates.

In this case, Gallagher has been elected with a surplus of 417 votes, so the next count consisted of the distribution of his surplus votes among the remaining candidates. The important point here is that not all of Gallagher's votes transfer; only that amount which is surplus to the quota, thus, 7,453 votes must remain in his pile. As an illustration of how this is done, we can look at how the transfer of Gallagher's votes to Fred Coll (independent) was calculated. When the ballot papers were sorted according to the number two preferences, a packet of votes was transferable to Coll. After the event, it is possible to work out that this packet amounted to some 227 votes, or 2.9 per cent of the total. The calculation of exactly how many of these 227 votes to transfer to Coll is as follows:

$$\text{Number of Gallagher's votes to be transferred} = \frac{\text{Number of Gallagher's surplus votes}}{\text{Number of Gallagher's votes}} \times \text{Number of votes that would transfer to Coll}$$

If we apply this formula, we arrive at the following result: $(417 \div 7,870) \times 227 = 12$ votes, i.e. 2.9 per cent of Gallagher's surplus (417). This process is repeated for each of the remaining candidates, and the results are shown in the second column of Table 6.1. At this stage we notice one of the rewards of STV for the political scientist. As Richard Sinnott (1995: 199) notes, STV is 'information-rich'. By studying the way in which votes are transferred between the candidates we can learn a lot about the relationships between candidates, about the links between parties and about the coalitional tendencies of voters. We will look at this in more detail in a moment, but to illustrate the point, it is useful to look at how the Fianna Fáil votes (of

Pat the Cope Gallagher) transferred in this case: 276 votes (66 per cent of the total) went to his running mate, Mary Coughlan; seventy-seven votes (19 per cent) transferred to Fine Gael; thirty-eight votes (9 per cent) went to Democratic Left; while the Sinn Féin candidate received just nine votes (2 per cent) and the independents between them seventeen votes (4 per cent).

The transfer of Gallagher's surplus was not sufficient to place any of the other candidates over the quota, so the reason for the next count (count three) was the elimination of the candidate with the least votes, John McCluskey of Sinn Féin (412 votes). This is a far simpler exercise than the transfer of a surplus, because in this case the candidate is being eliminated and all his votes can be transferred. Once again, this count did not result in the election of a candidate, and so the process of eliminating the weakest candidates continued, and did so again through counts four, five and six. The situation regarding the placement of candidates at the end of count six remained largely unchanged from that after count one. In other words, the top four candidates were arranged in the same order, as follows:

		Vote	Distance from quota
1	Pat the Cope Gallagher (Fianna Fáil)	ELECTED	
2	Mary Coughlan (Fianna Fáil)	7,317	− 136
3	Jim White (Fine Gael)	6,009	−1,444
4	Dinny McGinley (Fine Gael)	5,937	−1,516

Fianna Fáil was poised to win a second seat; Mary Coughlan required just 136 votes. The interesting battle was for the third seat. Only seventy-two votes separated White (6,009) and McGinley (5,937). The seventh count was once again an elimination, this time of Séamus Rodgers of Democratic Left (2,201 Votes). The greater number of his votes (873 votes; 40 per cent) were non-transferable. In other words, a high proportion of Rodger's voters were not prepared to declare any preference for Fianna Fáil or Fine Gael. Of those who were prepared to declare a preference, more of them did so for McGinley (651 votes; 30 per cent) than for White (370; 17 per cent); 307 (14 per cent) transferred to Mary Coughlan. The final result was a second seat for Fianna Fáil (Coughlan, with a surplus of 171 votes); and, in the event, the third seat was won by Dinny McGinley who just managed to overtake Jim White at the last moment. Note how

THE SINGLE TRANSFERABLE VOTE SYSTEM

McGinley was deemed elected without having actually reached the electoral quota – he was 865 votes short. The fact is, however, that there was no way that White (the only other remaining candidate) could overtake him. If the returning officer had wished, there could have been one more count to determine the final placement of Mary Coughlan's vote surplus of 171 votes, but since White was 209 votes behind McGinley, there was no way the 171 vote surplus could have made a difference, and so to carry out an extra count was un-necessary.

As this discussion suggests, an STV election count can take a long time; indeed, taking into account the possibility of recounts, it can sometimes take days before a final result is known. We have seen how the fortunes of candidates can change quite dramatically from one stage in the counting process to the next. There are two points worth noting about this. First, there is the fact that the STV system as used in Ireland (and Malta, though, as we shall see, not in Australia) contains an element of chance. Second, more generally the process of vote transfers can be crucial – indeed, this point is not lost on the party strategists seeking to maximize the gains for their parties.

The count in Dublin South-Central in 1992 provides a good illustration of the significance of the first point. On the final count (count thirteen) Ben Briscoe of Fianna Fáil was the fourth and final candidate to be elected with 6,526 votes (not reaching the quota of 8,049 votes). He had just five votes more than the candidate he beat, Eric Byrne (Democratic Left). Obviously the basic point is that Briscoe had more votes and therefore deserved to win. However, the reality is that Briscoe was possibly helped by an element of chance which is due to the way in which STV counts in Ireland (for lower house elections only) are administered. This relates to transfers of surplus votes. As we have seen, not all the votes are transferred; only those which are surplus to the quota. Once the returning officer has calculated which proportions of votes are to transfer to each of the remaining candidates, the problem then becomes one of determining which of the actual ballot papers are to be transferred and which are to remain in the pile. What happens at this stage varies between Ireland and Australia. In Ireland the returning officer simply picks the top ballot papers from each of the piles; in Australia the ballot papers are sorted according to all the remaining preferences and so the transfer (using fractions) takes adequate account of future vote transfers. The Irish case, therefore, incorporates an element of chance which could be significant whenever there is a close result (Gallagher and Unwin, 1986).

As Sinnott (1995: 199) notes: 'transfer patterns have potentially a lot to tell us about Irish voting behaviour'. The transfer patterns revealed by STV counts can provide fascinating insights into the relationships between particular candidates, the degree of faction fighting within a party and the views of voters towards certain coalition possibilities. In his seminal research on Irish transfer patterns from the 1920s to the 1970s, Michael Gallagher (1978) found a higher degree of voter 'loyalty' among Fianna Fáil supporters than among the supporters of the other parties. In other words Fianna Fáil voters were more likely to vote for all the party's candidates, rather than chopping and changing between candidates of other parties. This has important implications for vote management strategies because a party needs to maximize the efficiency of its vote. Candidate chances are threatened whenever the party cannot rely on the consistency of the transfers between its candidates.

Gallagher (1978) also found that Fianna Fáil supporters tend to be more 'exclusive' than the supporters of the other parties, i.e. they are more likely to plump only for Fianna Fáil candidates, not declaring any preferences for other candidates. On the one hand, plumping is potentially damaging for the party involved because its supporters are not making maximum use of the possibility to influence the election outcome; the best way for a voter to 'use' STV is to declare as many preferences as possible. On the other hand, as Sinnott (1995: 212) notes: 'from a party point of view . . . it is possible to argue that any losses involved in failing to affect the outcome by not transferring beyond the party are more than compensated for by encouraging the party supporters to think exclusively of the party and not to contemplate the possibility of giving even lower order preferences to another party. The presumed effect of this would be to strengthen the voters' loyalty to the party and minimize leakage or defection in future elections'.

The third set of patterns Gallagher identified in the period he studied related to transfers between candidates of different parties. In particular, given the fact that Fine Gael and Labour had formed coalition governments in the 1950s and again in the 1970s, it was interesting to examine the relationship between their respective supporters. In general there was some evidence of voter sympathy for the link between the two parties in the periods in question; however, the inter-party transfers tended to be higher from Fine Gael to Labour than vice versa.

Gallagher (1993) has also examined the transfer patterns in the 1992 election. He finds that in 1992 there was a marked drop in the levels of voter 'loyalty' or 'solidarity' among Fianna Fáil supporters, dropping from 83 per cent in the 1980s to 70 per cent in 1992 – the party's worst result since 1927. This reflects the fact that Fianna Fáil had been going through an unusually difficult period of internal indiscipline and faction fighting. Fine Gael's solidarity figure was even lower, just 65 per cent, its lowest since 1944.

The destinations of inter-party transfers in the 1992 election are shown in Table 6.2, which provides details only of those cases where specific pairs of parties had one or more candidates available to receive transfers. There are three distinct patterns worth noting. First, and most controversially, Labour supporters were more inclined to transfer their votes to Fine Gael candidates rather than to Fianna Fáil candidates, yet ultimately the Labour leader agreed to form a coalition government with Fianna Fáil. 'It would be difficult to argue from these figures that a coalition with Fianna Fáil is what Labour supporters were voting for' (Gallagher, 1993: 68). Ultimately, two years later, the voters finally did get their way when the coalition government collapsed and a new coalition government of Fine Gael, Labour and Democratic Left was formed mid-way. The second pattern to note in 1992 was how the Progressive Democrat (PD) supporters were more inclined to transfer to Fine Gael than to Fianna

Table 6.2 **Destinations of inter-party transfers in the Irish 1992 election**

Transfers from	Parties available in each constituency to receive transfers	Percentage of transfers received			
		FF	FG	PD	DL
Labour	Fianna Fáil, Fine Gael (24)	19.2	39.5		
Labour	Fine Gael, Dem. Left (13)		31.5		21.0
Labour	Fianna Fáil, Prog. Democrat (13)	14.9		13.8	
P. Democrat	Fianna Fáil, Fine Gael (8)	21.0	48.5		
Pro-Life	Fianna Fáil, Fine Gael (21)	30.8	23.2		

Notes: These figures refer to 'terminal' transfers, i.e. transfers from party A to party B when party A has no other candidates left in the race. The figures in parentheses show the number of cases where these terminal transfers arose.

Source: Gallagher (1993: Table 4.8).

Fáil, reflecting the similarities in the economic policies of both parties. The proportions of transfer were lower than in 1989, however (Gallagher, 1990), largely due to the fact that Fianna Fáil and the PDs were in coalition from 1989–92. Finally, the supporters of independent candidates promoting 'pro-life', i.e. anti-abortion, policies were more likely to transfer to Fianna Fáil, reflecting the more conservative stance of Fianna Fáil on this issue.

6.3 The consequences of STV for the political system

As we have seen, STV shares a number of features with the first past the post system – explaining its popularity among British electoral reformers. The country is divided into territorial constituencies, electing constituency politicians. The voters are asked to choose between candidates not (as in most list systems) parties. On the other hand, STV differs from FPTP in two significant respects: it is a proportional system, and there is more than one MP per constituency.

There are two themes we need to consider when assessing this (or other) electoral systems: how proportional it is, and what consequences it has for the political system generally. There has been much debate in the academic literature over how proportional STV is. This issue is dealt with in detail in chapter 7. As we shall see, conclusions vary widely: some argue that STV is one of the most proportional systems around, while others suggest that it is merely a semi-proportional system (Blondel, 1969; Gallagher, 1975; Lijphart, 1986; 1994; Taagepera and Shugart, 1989). For the most part, the former are dealing with theoretical comparisons between STV and list systems (in particular, ignoring the effects of a tendency for low district magnitudes in STV systems), the latter with practical comparisons. In chapter 7 the various electoral systems are assessed on the issue of proportionality; this section touches on a few of the themes of specific relevance to the STV system.

To repeat the exercise of earlier chapters, Table 6.3 lists the percentages of votes and seats for Irish parties in each election since 1951. As is evident from the columns listing the percentage differences between votes and seats, the system produces much more proportional results than is the case in FPTP or majoritarian systems. The vote–seat differences are never in double figures; they are

Table 6.3   Irish general elections, 1951–92: percentage votes and seats

	Fianna Fáil			Fine Gael			Labour		
	Vote (%)	Seat (%)	Diff. (%)	Vote (%)	Seat (%)	Diff. (%)	Vote (%)	Seat (%)	Diff. (%)
1951	46.3	46.9	+0.6	25.8	27.2	+1.4	11.4	10.9	–0.5
1954	43.4	44.2	+0.8	32.0	34.0	+2.0	12.1	12.9	+0.8
1957	48.3	53.1	+4.8	26.6	27.2	+0.6	9.1	8.2	–0.9
1961	43.8	48.6	+4.8	32.0	32.6	+0.6	11.6	11.1	–0.5
1965	47.7	50.0	+2.3	34.1	32.6	–1.5	15.4	15.3	–0.1
1969	45.7	52.1	+6.4	34.1	34.7	+0.6	17.0	12.5	–4.5
1973	46.2	47.9	+1.7	35.1	37.5	+2.4	13.7	13.2	–0.5
1977	50.6	56.8	+6.2	30.5	29.1	–1.4	11.6	11.5	–0.1
1981	45.3	47.0	+1.7	36.5	39.2	+2.7	9.9	9.0	–0.9
Feb. 1982	47.3	48.8	+1.5	38.0	48.8	+0.7	9.1	9.0	–0.1
Nov. 1982	45.2	45.2	—	42.2	45.2	+3.0	9.4	9.6	+0.2
1987	44.1	48.8	+4.7	30.7	48.8	+3.6	6.4	7.2	+0.8
1989	44.2	46.4	+2.2	33.1	46.4	+3.8	9.5	9.0	–0.5
1992	39.1	41.0	+1.9	27.1	41.0	+2.6	19.3	19.9	+0.6

	Progressive Democrats			Workers' Party/ Democratic Left			Green Party		
	Vote (%)	Seat (%)	Diff. (%)	Vote (%)	Seat (%)	Diff. (%)	Vote (%)	Seat (%)	Diff. (%)
1973				1.1	0.0	–1.1			
1977				1.7	0.0	–1.7			
1981				1.7	0.6	–1.1			
Feb. 1982				2.2	1.8	–0.4			
Nov. 1982				3.3	1.2	–2.1	0.2	0.0	–0.2
1987	11.8	8.4	–3.4	3.8	2.4	–1.4	0.4	0.0	–0.4
1989	5.5	3.6	–1.9	5.0	4.2	–0.8	1.5	0.6	–0.9
1992	4.7	6.0	+1.3	2.8	2.4	–0.4	1.4	0.6	–0.8

Note: Percentages may not add up to 100 because smaller parties and 'Others' have
    been excluded.
Sources: Mackie and Rose (1991); election results.

consistently smaller than in Tables 2.1, 3.2 or 3.3 (though, generally
not quite as small as in Tables 4.4, 4.5 or 5.1); smaller parties are,
comparatively speaking, not systematically cheated by the system.
Furthermore, there are few, if any, examples of the sorts of discrepancies over the formation of parliamentary majorities which were
noted in chapters 2 and 3. Indeed the only example worth noting is

the case of the 1973 election when Fianna Fáil lost seats (and government) despite having gained votes.

When dealing with the issue of proportionality, the factor of greatest significance – as indicated in the previous section – is constituency size (or district magnitude). If Hare's proposal of having all of the UK as one great constituency were followed, this would produce a highly proportional result, but at what cost? Imagine the unfortunate voter having to decide between thousands of candidates on a ballot paper which would be several metres long! An illustration of what this could mean is provided by an American example in the 1930s (Hermens, 1984). For a brief period, New York state adopted STV for municipal elections. In one case, in Brooklyn, the constituency was so large that 99 candidates put their names forward for election. The ballot paper was more than four feet long!

In short, there is a trade-off in the use of STV. The constituency needs to be large enough to produce as proportional a result as possible (i.e. to give candidates from all parties a fair chance), but it must not be so large that it makes the voters job of choosing between candidates impossible. It is generally accepted that the optimal size for STV constituencies is at least five seats (Taagepera and Shugart, 1989: ch. 11). In practice, in Malta and virtually all Australian STV elections, this requirement is met; in Ireland, however, a large proportion of the constituencies are three or four seats (Farrell *et al.*, 1996).

The Australians have devised one way of getting round the problem of over-long ballot papers. In Australian Senate elections the ballot paper is divided in two by a line: above the line all the party labels are displayed horizontally with a box next to each one; below the line there are lists of party candidates, each one grouped under the appropriate party label. This is more akin to the Malta ballot paper than to the Irish one, though, as we can see in Figure 6.3, what distinguishes the Australian ballot paper is the fact that the party labels are grouped horizontally instead of vertically. The voter can either fill out preferences for all the candidates (remember that in the case of Australian Senate elections all preferences must be completed for a vote to be counted as valid) or, alternatively, the voter can opt to vote 'above the line' by making a 'ticket vote'. In this case the voter simply places a '1' in the box of his or her preferred party. This means the voter is (tacitly) accepting the preference ranking of candidates which has been agreed beforehand among the parties.

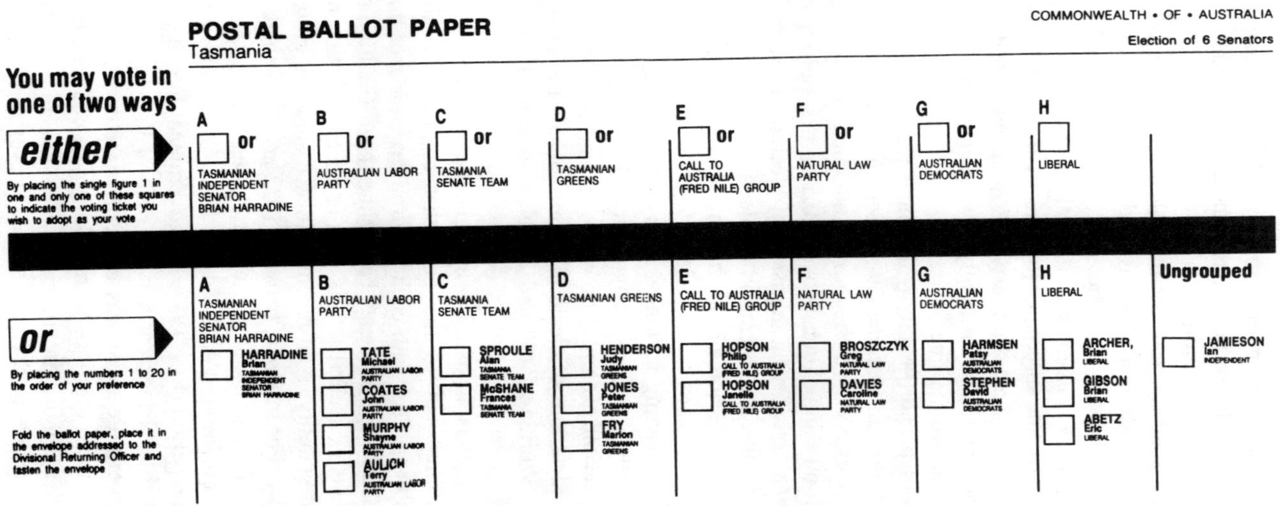
COMMONWEALTH • OF • AUSTRALIA
Election of 6 Senators

POSTAL BALLOT PAPER
Tasmania

You may vote in one of two ways

either

By placing the single figure 1 in one and only one of these squares to indicate the voting ticket you wish to adopt as your vote

A	B	C	D	E	F	G	H
☐ or	☐ or	☐ or	☐ or	☐ or	☐ or	☐ or	☐
TASMANIAN INDEPENDENT SENATOR BRIAN HARRADINE	AUSTRALIAN LABOR PARTY	TASMANIA SENATE TEAM	TASMANIAN GREENS	CALL TO AUSTRALIA (FRED NILE) GROUP	NATURAL LAW PARTY	AUSTRALIAN DEMOCRATS	LIBERAL

or

By placing the numbers 1 to 20 in the order of your preference

A	B	C	D	E	F	G	H	Ungrouped
TASMANIAN INDEPENDENT SENATOR BRIAN HARRADINE	AUSTRALIAN LABOR PARTY	TASMANIA SENATE TEAM	TASMANIAN GREENS	CALL TO AUSTRALIA (FRED NILE) GROUP	NATURAL LAW PARTY	AUSTRALIAN DEMOCRATS	LIBERAL	
☐ HARRADINE Brian TASMANIAN INDEPENDENT SENATOR BRIAN HARRADINE	☐ TATE Michael AUSTRALIAN LABOR PARTY	☐ SPROULE Alan TASMANIA SENATE TEAM	☐ HENDERSON Judy TASMANIAN GREENS	☐ HOPSON Philip CALL TO AUSTRALIA (FRED NILE) GROUP	☐ BROSZCZYK Greg NATURAL LAW PARTY	☐ HARMSEN Patsy AUSTRALIAN DEMOCRATS	☐ ARCHER, Brian LIBERAL	☐ JAMIESON Ian INDEPENDENT
	☐ COATES John AUSTRALIAN LABOR PARTY	☐ McSHANE Frances TASMANIA SENATE TEAM	☐ JONES Peter TASMANIAN GREENS	☐ HOPSON Janelle CALL TO AUSTRALIA (FRED NILE) GROUP	☐ DAVIES Caroline NATURAL LAW PARTY	☐ STEPHEN David AUSTRALIAN DEMOCRATS	☐ GIBSON Brian LIBERAL	
	☐ MURPHY Shayne AUSTRALIAN LABOR PARTY		☐ FRY Marion TASMANIAN GREENS				☐ ABETZ Eric LIBERAL	
	☐ AULICH Terry AUSTRALIAN LABOR PARTY							

Fold the ballot paper, place it in the envelope addressed to the Divisional Returning Officer and fasten the envelope

Figure 6.3 **Australian single transferable vote ballot paper**

In essence, what this amounts to is STV being treated as a list system but it does mean that there can be large ballot papers. For instance, in the 1995 election to the 21-member legislative council of the Australian state of New South Wales, there were twenty-seven parties fielding candidates. Like Brooklyn in the 1930s, there were ninety-nine candidates on the ballot paper which measured 1,000cm × 300cm. Given that turnout in Australian elections is compulsory, it is not surprising to learn that almost 94 per cent of voters turned out to vote. Similarly, the numbers of spoilt or invalid votes, at 6 per cent, was strikingly low because the bulk of voters opted to vote above the line.

The issue of proportionality – to which we return in chapter 7 – refers to the short-run or immediate effects of voting systems. Among the long-term effects which warrant attention are the number of parties, electoral competition between the parties and representation by MPs. When considering the issue of electoral reform, it is usual practice to examine the operation of electoral systems elsewhere to try to get an impression of the benefits and costs of the different systems. In the case of STV, Ireland is usually chosen as the case study, largely reflecting its long-established membership of the club of liberal democracies, its geographical location and its general familiarity. (Recent examples of where Ireland featured as the case study in considerations of electoral reform include the British Labour Party's Plant Working Party and the New Zealand Royal Commission.)

The basic criticisms of STV in Ireland relate to apparent party system instability and to the clientelist emphasis of the parliamentarians. Let us deal with each in turn. First, the fact that a large proportion of Irish governments have either been coalition or minority governments (Farrell, 1988) is seen to raise a question mark over governmental stability. And recent evidence suggests growing electoral instability. For instance, between 1932 and 1969 there were just four changes of government (i.e. either Fianna Fáil was in power, or there was a coalition dominated by Fine Gael and Labour). By contrast, in the period since 1973, the government has changed hands (or at least had to change partners) in each of the eight elections up to 1992. Furthermore there was a deeply unsettled period between 1981–2, when three elections were held in just eighteen months. By the end of the 1980s, the previously unthinkable had happened, Fianna Fáil – which in the past had only ever formed single-party governments – crossed the rubicon and (initially with deep reluctance) embraced coalition, first (in 1989), with the Progressive Democrats and then (in 1992), with Labour. Concomitant with the electoral shifts have been changes in the party system. What was once a textbook case of a 'two-and-a-half' party system (Fianna Fáil, Fine Gael and the small Labour party) had, by the mid-1980s, become a multi-party system with the entry of the Workers' Party (later essentially replaced by the Democratic Left), the Progressive Democrats and the Greens, all gaining Dáil (parliament) representation (Farrell, 1994; 1996).

When dealing with the issue of electoral stability in Ireland, the first point to be stressed is that while there may have been a large number of coalition and/or minority governments over the years, these have for the most part been long lasting (Farrell, 1988). In fact, on average Irish governments have tended to last for three- to four-year terms (including two periods when Fianna Fáil was in power for sixteen consecutive years from 1932–48 and again from 1957–73). There may have been a phase of governmental instability in 1981–2, but the fact is that it was a phase. Subsequent elections produced more decisive results. And, of course, such occurrences are not unique to Ireland – as evidenced by the two 1974 British elections, and also in 1979 by the collapse of the minority Labour government (which had been kept in office by a formal pact with the Liberals and various other less formal deals with minor parties).

As Table 6.3 shows, there may be more parties in the Irish system in the 1990s than there were in the 1970s, but the fact is that the three old parties remain predominant forces, and there is no certainty that the new parties will have a long-term future. (Ireland has had 'new' parties before.) In any event, why should we blame STV for this move towards multi-partyism? The fragmentation of the party system is a new feature to Irish politics, not a permanent fixture, yet the electoral system has remained unchanged since the 1920s. Furthermore, neither of the other countries where STV is used can be classified as multi-party: Malta has a two-party system (Zanella, 1990), and Australia has a two-bloc party system (Labor vs. the Liberal–National coalition), though smaller parties (notably the Democrats and the Greens) have managed to gain limited representation in the Senate (McAllister, 1992).

The second apparent problem with STV relates to how political life in Ireland is predominated by a brokerage style of politics.

Parliamentarians work their 'parish pumps', attracting votes by a heavy emphasis on constituency social work and localist concerns (for the literature on this, see Carty, 1981). More time seems to be spent in the Dáil signing letters to constituents and raising constituency matters in question time than with the weightier matters of national legislation. Surveys of TDs (MPs) reveal a heavy constituency workload (Roche, 1982; Whyte, 1966). Election campaigns are characterized by a similar emphasis on local issues and by regular faction fights between candidates of the same party. And there is good reason for the latter: between 1951 and 1977, for example, roughly one-third of the incumbent TDs who lost their seats were displaced by running mates from the same party (Carty, 1981: 114). In recent years that proportion seems to be rising (Gallagher, 1990; 1993).

The emphasis on localism is also evident among Irish voters. There is a well-established literature which explores the 'friends-and-neighbours' voting tendencies of the Irish electorate (Bax, 1976; Carty, 1981; Sacks, 1976). Candidates are found to receive more votes in that part of the constituency where they live, and there is a clear localist bias in voting behaviour, affecting the rank-ordering of candidates by the electorate. In recent years the parties' headquarters have sought to exploit this 'friends-and-neighbours' tendency with elaborate vote-management strategies, whereby candidates are picked from different corners of the constituency and voters in each locale are actively encouraged to vary the ordering of their preferences so as to maximize the efficiency of the party vote. The basic idea is that the more equal the spread of first preferences across the different party candidates, the greater the chance that more will be elected (see Farrell, 1994).

In each of these points about Irish localism, STV is usually credited with a key role: the heavy emphasis on constituency case-work, faction-fighting between candidates from the same party, a focus on constituency, localist matters in election campaigns and parliamentary work, and 'friends-and-neighbours' voting are all seen as resulting – at least in large part – from the candidate-centred, preference voting of STV (Carty, 1981; Farrell, 1985; Katz, 1980; Parker, 1983).

To what extent is Irish brokerage politics caused by STV and to what extent is the apparent relationship coincidental? The fact is that Irish political culture is personified by a high degree of localism

(Chubb, 1982; Schmitt, 1973) and it would be disingenuous to suppose that somehow this would dissipate if the electoral system were changed. It may be the case that multi-seat constituencies provoke competition between party candidates, but why should this take the form of competition over constituency work? As Michael Gallagher (1987: 32) has noted, there is nothing to prevent 'candidates of the same party trying fervently to establish reputations not as active constituency workers but as active parliamentarians'. Once again the international evidence does not support the linkage between STV and brokerage politics. A detailed comparison between Ireland and the Australian island state of Tasmania (the first place to use STV) finds little to support the claim that brokerage is caused by STV (O'Connell, 1983). A comparison of attitudes and backgrounds of the membership of the two Australian houses of parliament finds, if anything, a higher constituency emphasis among lower house members (elected under the alternative vote) than among upper house members (elected by STV) (Farrell and McAllister, 1995). Finally, a test of STV on London voters during the 1994 European Parliament election found little evidence of 'friends-and-neighbours' voting by the voters (Bowler and Farrell, 1994; 1996).

There are two more technical matters which warrant attention when dealing with STV. First, there is the issue of what are known as 'ballot position effects', in which it is suggested that a candidate's chances of being elected are influenced by where his or her name is located on the ballot paper. The second point – much stressed in the British Labour Party's Plant Report (Labour Party: 1993) – that STV can produce anomalous results. This latter point refers, in particular, to the issue of 'monotonicity', in which it is argued that, under STV, it is not necessarily always the case that a candidate's chances of being elected are helped by an increase in his or her share of the vote. We start with the first of these concerns.

Ballot position effects refer to the fact that voters are lazy or uninterested, that where possible voters may take short-cuts to reduce the effort involved in voting. Evidently voting can be a non-taxing exercise in some systems. For instance, in a British election a voter simply marks an 'X' next to the name of one candidate. In a Spanish election, as we saw in chapter 4, a voter chooses the ballot paper of his or her preferred party and simply drops it in the box. It is a quite different matter to require a voter to read through a list of, say, fifteen candidates and rank-order them. One obvious solution for the voter is to vote not in order of *preference*, but, instead, in order of *sequence*. The idea here is that voters read down (or possibly up) the list of candidate names and place a '1' next to the first name they recognize (or the first name from the party they support), a '2' next to the second, and so on. This is said to produce a biased result in favour of those candidates whose names start with letters at the beginning (or the end) of the alphabet, and accordingly it is generally referred to as 'alphabetical' voting. It has also been given such titles as 'bullet', or 'donkey', voting.

Politicians have been known to take this issue very seriously. For instance, in a celebrated case in the Australian Senate elections of New South Wales in 1937, the Labor party fielded four candidates whose surnames all happened to begin with 'A'; all four were elected. (Since 1940 the placement of Senate candidates has been determined by lot.) In Ireland, where politicians can quite easily change their name by deed poll, there were two cases in the 1980s of politicians who apparently sought to benefit from alphabetical voting, while at the same time attempting to advertise their particular issue concerns more widely. One candidate called Seán Loftus had his name altered to Seán Alderman Dublin Bay-Rockall Loftus; meanwhile a certain William Fitzsimon decided to change his name to William Abbey of the Holy Cross Fitzsimon. Of the two, Loftus was the only one to achieve any measure of success (briefly in 1981), but whether this had anything to do with the name change is a moot point.

Politicians are not the only ones to take ballot position effects seriously. Academics have been researching the issue for some time and, while there may be doubts over the accuracy of a number of these studies on the grounds of methodological weaknesses (Darcy and McAllister, 1990), there is none the less undoubted evidence that it does play a role in Australian and Irish elections (Kelley and McAllister, 1984; Robson and Walsh, 1974). However, if this is a problem (and a very small one at that), it is one with a simple solution – rotation of candidate names on the ballot paper (Darcy and Mackerras, 1993). The idea is relatively simple. The ordering of candidate names is changed at a number of stages during the printing of the ballot papers to ensure that each candidate has an equal chance of appearing at the top (and bottom). This has been the practice in parts of the United States for over forty years; Tasmania adopted it in 1980, and the Australian Capital Territory followed suit in 1994.

Among the criticisms of STV in the formal literature on voting

Table 6.4 **A hypothetical ordering of voter preferences in a preferential election**

Category of voter	No. of voters in the category	Preference ranking of candidates
I	7	Tom, Dick, Harry, Shirley
II	6	Dick, Tom, Harry, Shirley
III	5	Harry, Dick, Tom, Shirley
IV	3	Shirley, Harry, Dick, Tom

Note: Eleven votes required to win, i.e. majority.
Source: Based on Brams and Fishburn (1984: 150).

theory, the most common is that it is 'non-monotonic', that 'more first-place votes can hurt, rather than help, a candidate' (Brams and Fishburn, 1984: 151). The point is that in very specific circumstances STV can potentially produce a paradoxical result where a candidate can actually be harmed by a higher vote. Table 6.4 provides a hypothetical example of how a non-monotonic result could occur. Since the issue of non-monotonicity is shared by all preferential electoral systems, for the sake of simplicity the example refers to a single-seat constituency where a candidate requires a majority of votes in order to win the seat (i.e. the alternative vote system used in Australia, see chapter 3). In this example there are four candidates, Tom, Dick, Harry and Shirley, and an electorate of twenty-one voters. The voters have been grouped into four categories, based on the way in which they ranked each of the candidates. For example, the seven voters in category I ranked Tom as their first choice, Dick as their second, Harry as their third, and Shirley as their fourth.

Since none of the candidates has an overall majority of eleven votes, the count proceeds to the next stage, by the elimination of the candidate with the least votes – in this case, Shirley. Shirley's three votes all transfer to Harry who's vote tally now rises to eight. Still none of the remaining candidates has managed to accumulate a majority of the votes. It is now Dick's turn to be eliminated. All of his six votes transfer to Tom, giving him a grand total of thirteen votes, and so he is elected.

Before Tom and his supporters can start celebrating, however, Dick asks for a recount. On re-sorting the ballot papers it is discovered that the ballot papers of the category IV voters were incorrectly sorted. In fact, they had all placed Tom as their first preference. Instead of ranking the candidates as Shirley, Harry, Dick and Tom, the category IV voters had ranked them as Tom, Shirley, Harry and Dick. At first glance, it looked to Tom and his supporters as if the recount were merely going to confirm his victory, because he now had a greater number of first preference votes, an increase from seven to ten – just one short of an overall majority. The effect of the recount was to increase Tom's vote. Once the counting proceeded, however, it quickly became clear that, despite the fact that Tom's vote had risen, he was actually destined not to win the seat. Since Shirley was now found to have received no votes, the candidate with the least votes after count one was, in fact, Harry, with five votes. On his elimination, all five of his votes transferred to Dick, raising his vote tally to eleven, an overall majority. This hypothetical example shows how the non-monotonic nature of preferential electoral systems (including STV) can work against a candidate. In this case, the increase of Tom's vote served to lose him the seat.

In its final report, the Plant Working Party placed great emphasis on the potential for 'paradoxical results' as one reason why STV was not suitable for Britain. A key figure advising the Working Party on this point was the academic, Michael Dummett, who is on record as describing STV as 'the second worst electoral system ever devised' after the FPTP system (Dummett, 1992). Nobody denies the non-monotonic nature of STV, or for that matter, of other preferential systems, but how important is this? There is no evidence to suggest that it is a common occurrence. Indeed, the Chief Electoral Officer of Northern Ireland is quite categorical in his view that 'the experience of the use of STV in Northern Ireland over the past 22 years, involving a range of election types and sizes, reveals no evidence to support *in practice* the lack of monotonicity' (Bradley, 1995: 47, emphasis in the original). A recent statistical test of the issue has produced the prediction that, were STV to be used in the UK, there would be 'less than one incidence every century of monotonicity failure' (Allard, 1995: 49).

Furthermore, it has been pointed out that even if non-monotonicity can on some occasions produce an unfair STV election result, surely, on the scale of things, the overall election result is *always* going to be fairer than under FPTP or the majoritarian 'supplementary vote' system which the Plant Working Party has recommended for Britain. Of course, the other point is that non-monotonicity is a feature of all preferential systems, including the 'supplementary vote'; therefore, it is somewhat ironic that the Plant Working Party used it as a reason to reject one preferential system in favour of another!

6.4 Is STV an appropriate system for Britain?

The Labour Party's Plant Working Party (Labour Party, 1993: ch. 2) was not enamoured of STV, judging it as technically flawed (i.e. the issue of monotonicity), politically inappropriate (because it 'can lead to' clientelism) and culturally unsuitable (because it would 'dilute' the constituency basis of British politics). It is possible, as we have seen, to take issue with each of these points; however, ultimately a theoretical debate on the pros and cons of STV becomes nothing more than a matter of taste.

In reality the only way to ever know if STV is suitable is to actually see it in operation. Dunleavy *et al.* (1992) have simulated an STV election in Great Britain, providing a useful basis for comparison with the actual 1992 election results. They divided the country into 123 multi-seat constituencies – for the most part five-seaters – instead of the actual 634 single-seat constituencies. As Table 6.5 shows, if the 1992 election had been fought using STV, this would have resulted in no party having an overall majority, requiring the formation of a coalition government. The Conservative Party would have lost most (eighty seats) in this election; Labour would have lost twenty-one seats, and the main beneficiaries would have been the Liberal Democrats (winning 102 seats).

Table 6.5 Parties' seats in Britain under STV compared with the 1992 FPTP election result: the Rowntree/ICM survey

	No. of seats	Con.	Lab.	Lib./ Dem.	Green	SNP/PC
South	260	123	74	57	6	0
North and Midlands	264	106	127	31	0	0
Scotland	72	18	31	7	0	16
Wales	38	9	18	7	0	4
Britain	634	256	250	102	6	20
Actual result in 1992	634	336	271	20	0	7
Net change in seats		−80	−21	+82	+6	+13

Source: Derived from Dunleavy *et al.* (1992: Table 10).

The Liberal Democrat result is not surprising, since that party can only gain from *any* form of PR system. According to Dunleavy *et al.*, what is surprising is how well Labour performs, winning almost as many seats as the Conservatives despite having 8 per cent fewer votes. There is evidence, they suggest, of an 'anti-Conservative and pro-Labour effect', due to a combination of 'multiple preferences, the local constituency arrangement, and the patterns of regional and local support' (Dunleavy *et al.*, 1992: 13). The crucial point, in their eyes, is that STV 'can deliver significantly distorted seat allocations, depending on how regional and local voting patterns are structured'. What they are referring to is the way in which STV results, in the latter part of the count, can turn on very small numbers of votes – as we saw in the Irish example above. They conclude, therefore, that 'STV is only contingently proportional'.

Two points can be made in disagreement with the argument of Dunleavy and his colleagues. First, it is possible that the pro-Labour bias was a quirk of one particular election. As we saw in Table 6.3, there are occasions when STV can produce somewhat anomalous results. However, this occurs far less frequently and far less distinctly than under FPTP, as Table 2.3 indicates. This relates to the second point of disagreement with Dunleavy *et al*. The basic fact is that when a comparison is drawn between the results of an FPTP election and an STV election, the STV result is far more proportional. Table 6.6 demonstrates this by comparing the percentage seat–vote differences under both systems (see the two columns of figures in bold). At no stage does the STV simulation come even close to having a two-digit difference between the percentage of votes a party receives and the percentage of seats it is awarded. In particular STV produces a much fairer result for the Liberal Democrats. And, crucially, while there is evidence of a slight bias in favour of Labour (+4.2 per cent), this is *less* than the bias Labour actually benefited from in the real election (+7.5 per cent). In other words the 1992 election under FPTP actually produced a greater pro-Labour bias than would have been achieved under STV.

Apart from the question of what electoral result is produced by STV, it is also interesting to examine how the ballot paper is used by the voters, assessing such issues as whether voters are more or less likely to switch from one party to another in later preferences, and how such tendencies may vary across different types of voters. In their 1992 study, Dunleavy *et al.* (1992: 10) found that just over half

Table 6.6   **Vote and seat percentage differences: comparing STV and FPTP in the British 1992 election**

	STV simulation Seat (%)	**Diff.** (%)	1992 election Vote (%)	**Diff.** (%)	1992 election Seat (%)
Conservative	40.4	**−2.4**	42.8	**+10.2**	53.0
Labour	39.4	**+4.2**	35.2	**+7.5**	42.7
Liberal Democrat	16.1	**−2.2**	18.3	**−15.1**	3.2
Green Party	0.9	**+0.4**	0.5	**−0.5**	0.0
SNP/Plaid Cymru	3.2	**+0.8**	2.4	**−1.3**	1.1

Note: Not including Northern Ireland.
Source: Dunleavy *et al.* (1992); election returns.

of the respondents voted for more than one party, i.e. at some stage in their vote, the respondents declared a preference for a candidate from a second party. A closer examination reveals that this tended to happen in the lower preferences and it was more common among supporters of smaller parties. So while about 90 per cent of Conservative and Labour respondents gave their first preference to a candidate from the same party that they had supported in the 1992 election, the corresponding figure for Liberal Democrat respondents was just over 70 per cent. The respective proportions dropped in the case of second preference votes to 65 per cent and 51 per cent, and in third preferences to 54 per cent and 45 per cent.

The tendency to vote for more than one party was greater among younger voters (Dunleavy *et al.*, 1993: 184–5). This is consistent with the fact that younger voters are generally more volatile. There were also distinct regional differences: multiple choices were most common in the Highlands, Eastern Scotland and Wales; least common in East Anglia and the North. Class differences produced no significant effects in voting patterns.

6.5 Conclusion

STV has a lot to recommend it. Of all systems it goes furthest towards removing the power of the party elites to determine which of their candidates are elected. Under FPTP a voter can only vote for the one party candidate nominated. Under fixed list systems, the voter cannot even vote for candidates: the rank-ordering is determined by the party elite who drew up the lists. In contrast, STV gives the voter great scope 'to choose between candidates on personal as well as party grounds, and his choice overrides that of any party organization' (Lakeman, 1970: 140). In this sense it can be judged a highly democratic system.

In terms of the points usually raised in the British debate about electoral reform (see chapter 2), STV seems to fit all the necessary requirements. First, it incorporates a central role for constituency representation. More than that, in most cases it actually permits the possibility that voters for the main parties will have one (or two) constituency representatives they can approach – the problem of 'safe' Labour or 'safe' Conservative seats should not arise. Second, there is no evidence to suggest that a move towards STV should necessarily lead to greater electoral or governmental instability; certainly it has not tended to be a problem for those countries currently using STV.

Third, while the counting procedures may be more complex and long-winded, the actual process of voting should not present any great difficulties for the average voter. For instance, with one exception, there is no significant evidence of any greater number of spoiled votes in STV systems. The exception is Australia which traditionally has had high numbers of spoiled, or 'informal' votes, and with good reason (McAllister and Makkai, 1993). Australian voters have to contend with a confusing array of electoral systems for the different levels of elections, combined with a national tendency for regular electoral reform (perhaps only France alters its electoral system more frequently). Furthermore, the voters are expected, by law, to turn out to vote. And, prior to 1984, they were also forced to fill out every preference on the Senate ballot paper. The introduction of 'ticket voting' in 1984 – when voters were given the option of simply marking one preference against their favoured party, letting the rank-ordering be decided by the party elite – did much to reduce the level of spoiled votes.

There are two other points in support of the argument that STV is simple to use. First, in the cases where it has been experimented with in 'mock-ballot surveys' in Britain, the respondents appear to have had little difficulty in mastering it. Second, it has a popular following in those countries where it is currently been used. For instance, as we have seen, on two occasions the Irish voters were asked in a referendum whether they would like to replace STV with FPTP. On both occasions, the answer was 'No'.

There are a lot of points that can be made in support of STV, however, it suffers from one major problem: the fact that 'it has been used in so few countries [means] that possible problem areas may remain untested' (Taagepera and Shugart, 1989: 237). Technical problems (such as non-monotonicity) could turn out to be serious, though this is unlikely. There is also the question of constituency size. It might be argued that what works in Ireland and Malta (and, with some significant amendments, in Australia), may not necessarily work so well in, say, Britain, France or Germany. However, is there really any reason to suppose that population size should matter? Surely, STV can work just as easily in a system with 130 five-seat constituencies as it does in one with thirty five-seat constituencies, and therefore it is hardly very relevant to invoke a size argument as one reason why not to employ STV in the UK or other heavily populated system.

Note

[1] Arguably the origins of STV can be traced back even further, to the writings of Thomes Wright Hill (1763–1851; a mathematician). However, the system he proposed lacked many of the features of STV (Hart, 1992: 6–9).

7

THE POLITICAL CONSEQUENCES OF ELECTORAL SYSTEMS

Electoral systems have political consequences. The truth of this statement is revealed in the burgeoning literature on electoral systems, which seeks to show precisely what these consequences are. This chapter explores the main findings of these studies, addressing the major points of disagreement between the authors. There are a number of consequences of electoral systems which we need to consider, among them: the effects on proportionality, on numbers of parties, and on the representation of women and minorities. These are dealt with in the first three sections.

In combination, these three consequences are said to play a major role in determining the overall stability of the system. As was discussed in chapter 1, it is usual to argue that, in choosing an electoral system, we face a trade-off: either the electoral system is proportional – facilitating the entry of minor parties and the representation of minority interests – and produces a situation where the governmental system is unstable, or the electoral system is non-proportional and the governmental system is much more stable. In section 7.4 we examine the extent to which this perception of a necessary trade-off is correct.

In addition to the macro-level effects of electoral systems, which in some part are all related to the issue of their proportionality profiles, in recent years there has been increasing attention to the micro-level effects of electoral system, in terms of both how voters use them (e.g. strategic and split-ticket voting) and how parties are affected by them (e.g. variations in campaign style). Here, the attention is less on the question of proportionality (for the most part affected by district magnitude and electoral formula) and its consequences, and more on the issue of the mechanics of the vote, which, is affected mainly by ballot structure. These micro-level effects of electoral systems are considered in section 7.5. The chapter closes off, in section 7.6, with a discussion on the politics of electoral reform.

7.1 Proportionality profiles of different electoral systems

How proportional are proportional representation (PR) systems? The principal advantage which PR systems are supposed to have over non-PR systems is that, on average, they produce more proportional results, i.e. they minimize the distortion between the number of votes a party wins and the number of seats it ends up with in parliament. The previous chapters provided evidence in support of this. When we looked at the percentage differences between votes and seats, the ranking between the different systems appeared to tally with expectations, i.e. first past the post (FPTP) and the majoritarian systems produced the largest percentage differences; single transferable vote (STV), list and the two-votes systems produced the smallest.

It is now time to produce more systematic evidence, to apply a more rigorous test across a wide range of different electoral systems in various countries over a long period of time. This way we can get a true picture not only of whether PR systems produce more proportional results than non-PR systems, but also about which PR system is the more proportional.

Of course, things are not as easy as they may seem. The comparative assessment of the proportionality of electoral systems has been dominated by a series of debates (sometimes rancorous) over methodology: first, on the issue of which factors most affect levels of proportionality, and second, on the issue of which is the most appropriate index to adopt. Given the disagreement over measuring techniques, there should be little surprise that this produces different rankings for the various electoral systems.

For the most part, questions about the factors influencing proportionality revolve around the three main dimensions of electoral systems which have been discussed throughout this study: electoral formula, district magnitude and ballot structure. The seminal work by Douglas Rae in the 1960s produced the following findings: electoral formula has an effect on proportionality, district magnitude has an even greater effect and ballot structure has no effect. There has been little disagreement with these general conclusions, although Lijphart (1994) has recently found some evidence that ballot structure might be influential. Lijphart also adds other factors to the list of influences on proportionality, of which the most significant is assembly size, with larger parliaments being statistically associated with higher degrees of proportionality.

There is general agreement that district magnitude is 'the decisive factor' in determining proportionality (Taagepera and Shugart, 1989: 112; also Lijphart, 1994). There is far greater uncertainty about how to rank the different electoral formulae. In particular, there is a problem over how to include STV in any evaluation. As Lijphart (1986) has observed, for this reason many simply ignore STV altogether and focus instead on the list systems. Here there is general agreement that the largest remainder systems are the most proportional, followed by Sainte-Laguë, then d'Hondt (Lijphart, 1986; Loosemore and Hanby, 1971; Rae, 1967; see chapter 4, pp. 62–68, for descriptions of these systems).

The problems with assessing the proportionality of STV are twofold. First, the relatively low level of district magnitude (at least as used in Ireland, which is the usual focus of attention, and whose constituencies are never more than five seats), means that STV tends to be labelled less proportional, or – as the phrase goes – 'quasi-proportional' (Taagepera and Shugart, 1989: 207; Katz, 1984). One way around this problem is simply to ignore district magnitude and instead to focus on the theoretical aspects of how the different electoral formulae vary over proportionality. This is the approach adopted by Jean Blondel (1969); however, his conclusion that STV is the most proportional of the PR systems (and that largest remainder is the least) has not found general support.

The second problem with STV is that quintessentially it is a candidate-based system: unlike the list systems where voters are choosing between different parties, under STV voters choose between different candidates on the ballot paper. There are difficulties, therefore, in assessing STV with measures of proportionality which are based on vote and seat shares for *parties* (see Gallagher, 1975; Mair and Laver, 1975). In consequence, as Rae (1967: 38) notes: '[i]t is not quite clear how this arrangement is likely to compare with other PR formulae'. And, rather than attempting a specific rank for STV, Rae (1967: 111) can only conclude that 'in general, [it] behaves like any other sort of proportional representation. It operates quite proportionally'. Lijphart (1994:159; 1986) suggests a way around the problem. He makes the 'simplifying assumption' that voters cast their votes entirely within party lines (which is pretty much the case in Malta), and that therefore the vote can be construed as a 'party vote'. This leads to the following ranking of the main PR formulae, from most to least proportional:

- Largest remainder-Hare; Sainte-Laguë.
- Largest remainder-Droop; STV; modified-Sainte-Laguë.
- D'Hondt; largest remainder-Imperiali.

This ranking is based on a theoretical assessment of the likely electoral outcomes from using each of these formulae. The problem next becomes one of how to assess the degree to which reality matches up with theory. Prima facie, it might appear a relatively straightforward exercise to plot the trends in proportionality for each of these formulae across a range of countries over time. In fact, it is not so simple for two main reasons: first, we need access to a suitable measure, or index, of proportionality, and second, we need a ranking which can take account of all the possible influences on proportionality, not just electoral formula, but also district magnitude and other lesser influences like assembly size. Both of these issues have featured prominently in the literature on electoral system effects (for a recent review, see Lijphart, 1994).

Over the years, a number of different measures of proportionality have been developed by Rae (1967 – the Rae index), Loosemore and Hanby (1971 – the Loosemore-Hanby index), Gallagher (1991 – the Least-squares index), and Lijphart (1994 – the Largest-deviation index). They will not be discussed here. In his comprehensive overview, Lijphart (1994: 67) finds that all four indices are 'highly and significantly correlated', but he has a clear preference for Gallagher's Least-squares index.[1] Table 7.1 makes use of the Least-squares index to rank the proportionality of electoral systems used in

Table 7.1 Levels of disproportionality and the effective number of parties under different electoral systems

Rank and country	Electoral formula	District magnitude[c]	Period	No. of elections	Level of disproportionality	Effective no. of parties
1. Germany	LR-Hare[a]	497	1987	1	0.67	3.47
2. Israel	LR-Hare	120	1951–69	6	0.86	4.92
3. Netherlands	d'Hondt	100–50	1946–89	14	1.31	4.59
4. Austria	LR-Hare[b]	20.3	1971–90	6	1.43	2.42
5. Italy	LR-Droop/Imperiali[b]	17.9	1946	1	1.56	4.39
6. Sweden	modified Sainte-Laguë[a]	349.3	1970–88	7	1.67	3.40
7. Denmark	LR-Hare[a]	148.5–75	1945–88	19	1.80	4.52
8. Sweden	modified Sainte-Laguë	8.3	1952–68	6	2.36	3.11
8. Switzerland	d'Hondt	8.2	1947–87	11	2.36	5.10
9. Germany	d'Hondt[a]	36.6–496.9	1949–83	10	2.50	3.19
10. Israel	d'Hondt	120	1949, 1973–88	6	2.59	3.97
11. Italy	LR-Imperiali[b]	19.6	1958–87	8	2.71	3.62
12. Finland	d'Hondt	13.2	1945–87	13	2.86	5.03
13. Luxembourg	d'Hondt	14	1945–89	10	3.11	3.30
14. Belgium	d'Hondt[a]	23.5	1946–87	15	3.23	4.63
15. Ireland	STV	3.8	1948–92	15	3.43	3.52
16. Sweden	d'Hondt	8.2	1948	1	3.51	3.06
17. Austria	LR-Droop[b]	6.6	1945–70	8	3.61	2.25
18. Italy	reinforced LR-Imperiali[b]	18.8	1948–53	2	3.64	3.06
19. Norway	modified Sainte-Laguë[a]	165	1989	1	3.65	4.23
20. Malta	STV	5–5.1	1947–81	10	3.76	2.47

21. Greece	LR-Droop[b]	5.1	1989–90	3	4.06	2.36
22. Costa Rica	LR-Hare	6.4–8.1	1953–90	10	4.07	2.43
23. Portugal	d'Hondt	12.4	1975–87	7	4.25	3.05
24. Norway	modified Sainte-Laguë	7.8	1953–85	9	4.38	3.26
25. Iceland	d'Hondt[a]	52–60.3	1946–87	14	4.52	3.70
26. USA	FPTP	1	1946–90	23	5.41	1.92
27. Japan	limited vote	4–9	1946–90	18	5.74	3.04
28. France	d'Hondt	5.8	1986	1	7.23	3.90
29. Norway	d'Hondt	7.5	1945–49	2	8.53	2.93
30. Australia	majoritarian	1	1946–93	20	8.84	2.49
31. Spain	d'Hondt	6.7	1977–89	5	8.95	2.72
32. UK	FPTP	1	1945–92	14	10.76	2.51
33. New Zealand	FPTP	1	1946–93	17	11.11	1.96
34. Greece	d'Hondt[a]	5.3–6.7	1974–85	4	11.21	2.08
35. Canada	FPTP	1	1945–88	15	11.33	2.37
36. France	majoritarian	1	1958–81, 1988	8	13.86	3.45
37. India	FPTP	1–1.2	1952–84	8	17.76	2.15

Notes: [a] A two-tiered electoral system. In this case the higher level is decisive so this has been selected (see Lijphart, 1994: Table 2.5).
[b] A two-tiered electoral system. In this case the lower tier is decisive so this has been selected (see Lijphart, 1994: Table 2.4).
[c] Wherever the district magnitude changes, the range is provided here.

The countries have been ranked according to different levels of disproportionality. The disproportionality index used is the Least-squares index developed by Gallagher (1991; Lijphart, 1994: 60–1). It is calculated as follows: square the vote–seat differences for each party (ignoring 'others'); sum them; divide the total by two; and then take the square root. The index of effective number of parliamentary parties was derived by Laakso and Taagepera (1979; Lijphart, 1994: 67ff.). It is calculated as follows: 1 divided by the sum of the squared percentage seats for each party.

For the most part, these data are available in Lijphart (1994; appendix B). I am grateful to Arend Lijphart for having made available his more detailed tables of statistics on disproportionality and party system trends per country per election. Wherever possible the data have been updated to take account of recent elections.

Sources: Lijphart (1994); electoral returns.

twenty-seven democracies over the post-war period. (Strictly speaking, the ranking is of levels of 'disproportionality': those countries with lowest levels of disproportionality are located towards the top.)

One thing to note immediately from Table 7.1 is how, on a number of occasions, a country has more than one entry, indicating that the electoral formula has been changed. In truth, if we were to take account of all possible electoral changes (e.g. including such factors as ballot structure or assembly size; see Lijphart, 1994) we would have a substantially more complex table. Given the importance of district magnitude for overall proportionality, this is also provided in the table. In chapter 1, reference was made to Dieter Nohlen's assertion that 'fundamental' electoral system change is rare, occurring only 'in extraordinary historical situations' (Nohlen, 1984: 218). In chapter 5, we saw how this 'rule' required some qualification, especially given the dramatic processes of electoral reform in established democracies like Italy, Japan and New Zealand. In Table 7.1, however, it is evident that electoral system change (albeit not necessarily 'fundamental') is even more widespread than many may believe.

When we look, first, at the different electoral formulae, in some respects the ranking in Table 7.1 works pretty much as expected. The non-proportional systems (FPTP, the majoritarian systems and Japan's former limited vote system) are the least proportional systems, located in the bottom third grouping in the table. Largest remainder-Hare is the most proportional system, for the most part located in the top third grouping. (Sainte-Laguë does not appear anywhere in the table because, apart from its recent adoption by New Zealand, it has not been used since the Scandinavian countries moved over to modified-Sainte-Laguë; see chapter 4, p. 64.) STV also fits the ranking predicted by Lijphart: the Irish and Malta cases are both located in the middle grouping of countries. Research on STV in Australia (Senate and state elections) also places that country in the middle ranking (Farrell et al., 1996).

Ranking the remaining electoral systems – largest remainder-Droop, modified-Sainte-Laguë, d'Hondt and largest remainder-Imperiali – is less easy, reflecting the effects of variations in district magnitude, two-tier districting (see chapter 4, p. 69) and other factors which influence overall proportionality. For instance, the third place ranking for the Netherlands – a d'Hondt system – while against expectations, is understandable when we remember the particularly large district magnitude which is used (see p. 68). The Israeli case is instructive. A combination of largest remainder-Hare and a very large district magnitude ensured that country's number two ranking throughout the 1950s and 1960s. Its overall ranking slipped to number ten on the list with the switch to d'Hondt in the 1970s.

In general, the ranking of electoral systems with regard to district magnitude (or constituency size) also tallies well with expectations, as shown most accurately by the location of all the single-member countries, i.e. those with a district magnitude of one, at the bottom of the table. In his detailed and sophisticated analysis of this evidence, Lijphart (1994: 110) finds district magnitude to have the greatest effect on overall proportionality.

As Douglas Rae (1967) observes, the proportionality of different electoral systems relates to their short-term or 'proximal', effects. Electoral systems also have 'distal' or long-run, effects, as revealed by the numbers of parties in the political system and the representation of women and minorities. The next two sections deal with each of these in turn.

7.2 Electoral systems and party systems

We might expect – almost by definition, as it were – that electoral systems which are more proportional should coincide with more fragmented party systems. In the 1950s the French political scientist, Maurice Duverger (1954), put forward the proposition that non-proportional electoral systems (he referred specifically to FPTP) 'favour' two-party systems, while proportional electoral systems 'favour' multi-party systems. There are two parts to this argument which can be summarized by looking at the case of non-proportional electoral systems. First, there is the fact that, because it is more difficult for smaller parties to win seats under non-PR systems, the *mechanics* of these systems are bound to result in fewer parties in parliament. Second, there is also a *psychological* aspect, in the sense that voters are aware of the fact that a vote for a smaller party is a wasted vote and therefore they are less inclined to bother voting for them, thereby further compounding the difficulties for smaller parties (Blais and Carty, 1991).

Duverger's propositions have spawned a fascinating debate between political scientists over the issue of whether they should be considered to have law-like status (for a sample, see Duverger, 1986; Riker, 1986; Sartori, 1986). The main point at issue is that of causality: is multi-partism a consequence or a cause of proportionality? For instance, there are plenty of historical examples of multiparty systems which preceded the decision to opt for a PR electoral system, among them are Belgium, Denmark, Germany and Norway.

While clearly there is a 'chicken and egg' problem over causality, this should not distract us from the fact that wherever there is a proportional electoral system there is a greater likelihood of finding more parties represented in the parliament, and wherever there is a non-proportional electoral system, we are more likely to find a two-party system. Obvious examples of the latter include the US Congress, dominated by the Republicans and the Democrats, and the UK House of Commons, dominated by the Conservatives and Labour. Of course, given that in the British case there are clearly more than two parties in the parliament – in fact, currently there are nine! – this indicates the need for appropriate 'counting rules' for parties.

Markku Laakso and Rein Taagepera have devised an index which measures the 'effective' number of parties, based on the number of parties in parliament and their different sizes.[2] Using this index, for instance, the UK party system can be characterized as a '2.51-party system', reflecting the vote of the Liberal Democrats and the various Nationalist parties. The final column in Table 7.1 gives the scores across a range of countries. While there are cases where we find more parties than would be expected (e.g. non-proportional France with 3.45 parties) or fewer parties than expected (e.g. proportional Austria with 2.42 parties), for the most part the scores fit in well with expectations. The most proportional systems – those located in the top third of the table – average about four parties in parliament; those countries located in the middle grouping of the table average 3.2 parties, and the least proportional systems average 2.6 parties. In general, over the post-war period, those countries using non-proportional electoral systems average 2.3 parties, while the PR countries average 3.6 parties (Gallagher et al, 1995: 289; Lijphart, 1994: 96).

7.3 The representation of women

There are a number of steps which can be taken to resolve the evident problem of the underrepresentation of women (and other categories of voters) in a political system. For instance, in 1993 the British Labour

Party introduced quota rules on the nomination of women candidates, forcing certain constituency parties to have all-women shortlists in the event of a vacancy. Similar steps have been taken by parties in other countries (Norris, 1994). The Labour Party quota rules proved controversial and, after a successful court challenge, were subsequently dropped in 1996. Quota rules have also been used to ensure the better representation of minority groupings. An alternative method is to provide a certain number of parliamentary seats for minorities, as is the case of the Maori seats in New Zealand (Lijphart, 1986a). Another example was in Ireland in the 1920s and 1930s when the upper house of the parliament included a number of seats for Protestants, designed as a means of placating the minority population in what was predominantly a Catholic state. As was suggested in chapter 4, one other mechanical approach available in PR list systems (particularly with closed lists) is to place a certain number of women or minority candidates high on the party list and thereby ensure that more of them will be successfully elected (Darcy et al., 1994). The remainder of this section deals with the issue of women's representation which has tended to attract most attention.

We saw in the previous section how proportionality affected the number of parties in a system. In similar fashion, there is good reason to expect that the representation of women is also affected by the degree of proportionality of an electoral system. For instance, in recent research on the issue of women's representation, Pippa Norris (1996) has identified a 'modest increase' in the proportion of women MPs in all western democracies, the greatest increase being in proportional systems. She finds a relationship between proportionality and women's representation. All democracies where women comprise at least a quarter of the parliamentary membership use PR list electoral systems, with district magnitude having the greatest effect on women's representation.

Table 7.2 shows a clear relationship between the proportionality of the electoral system and the number of women legislators in the parliament: in general, the lowest representation of women is in those systems ranked low on the index of proportionality. The average representation of women is 16.9 per cent: in PR systems this rises to 20 per cent; in non-PR system it plummets to 10.4 per cent. Inevitably there are some countries where the representation of women is lower or higher than would be expected. For instance, the higher than average proportion of women legislators in non-

Table 7.2 **Women legislators in the lower house**

Country	Electoral formula	Year	Women MPs (%)	PR ranking[c]
Sweden	modified Sainte-Laguë[a]	1994	40.3	6
Norway	modified Sainte-Laguë[a]	1993	39.4	19
Finland	d'Hondt	1991	39.0	12
Denmark	LR-Hare[a]	1990	33.0	7
Netherlands	d'Hondt	1994	31.3	3
Germany	LR-Hare[a]	1994	26.3	1
Austria	LR-Hare[b]	1990	21.3	4
New Zealand	FPTP	1993	21.2	33
Canada	FPTP	1993	18.0	35
Switzerland	d'Hondt	1991	17.5	8
Spain	d'Hondt	1993	16.0	31
Italy	LR-Imperiali[b]	1994	15.1	11
Costa Rica	LR-Hare	1994	14.0	22
Ireland	STV	1992	12.1	15
USA	FPTP	1994	10.8	26
Belgium	d'Hondt[a]	1991	9.4	14
Israel	d'Hondt	1992	9.2	10
UK	FPTP	1992	9.2	32
Portugal	d'Hondt	1991	8.7	23
Australia	majoritarian	1993	8.2	30
India	FPTP	1991	7.3	37
France	majoritarian	1993	6.1	36
Greece	LR-Droop[b]	1993	6.0	21
Japan	limited vote	1993	2.7	27
Malta	STV	1992	1.5	20
Average			16.9	

Notes: [a] A two-tiered electoral system. In this case the higher level is decisive so this has been selected (see Lijphart, 1994: Table 2.5).
[b] A two-tiered electoral system. In this case the lower tier is decisive so this has been selected (see Lijphart, 1994: Table 2.4).
[c] For details on the PR ranking, see Table 7.1.
Sources: Table 7.1; Lane (1995); Lijphart (1994); Norris (1996).

proportional New Zealand reflects that country's use of party quotas. Canada is also higher than expected, reflecting a high turnover in the membership of the parliament (Norris, 1996).

The rather disappointing record in Ireland, with just 12.1 per cent women MPs, and, even more spectacularly, the Malta figure of 1.5

per cent women MPs have led some authors to speculate on whether STV might be less effective than other PR systems in promoting the representation of women (Hirczy, 1995; Lane, 1995). In fact, research tends to suggest that it is not so much STV as an electoral system which is to blame for this low proportion of women legislators; rather, it stems from 'the failure of party elites to recruit them in greater numbers' (Lane, 1995: 152). In other words, it is not the electoral system which is at fault so much as the party selection committees (also Kelley and McAllister, 1983).

Not only do proportional systems increase the chances for women to gain adequate representation in parliament, there is also evidence of a possible spillover effect in terms of the general promotion of women's interests, though we should be cautious about attaching too much importance to this. In his comprehensive review of the evidence, Arend Lijphart (1994a: 6) has found that 'better representation of women appears to result in better advancement of their interests [in terms] . . . of the quality of family policy'. He refers to an index of family policy which has been developed by the political sociologist, H. L. Wilensky, where, on a scale of 0–12 (the maximum score), the average score for non-PR systems in the postwar years is 2.5; the average score for PR systems is 7.9.

7.4 A possible trade-off: does greater proportionality imply greater instability?

In the previous three sections we have seen a great deal of evidence to support the contention that PR systems tend to produce more proportional results. In general, parliaments elected under proportional electoral systems tend to be more representative of society than is the case for those parliaments elected under non-proportional systems. This can also be seen in terms of the number of parties in the parliament and in the representation of women.

While few would dispute that having a more representative assembly is a good thing, there is considerable dispute over the degree to which such an assembly can operate effectively. As we saw earlier, this issue is usually presented in terms of a trade-off: either you can have a representative parliament which elects a similarly representative government, or you can have strong and stable government; you cannot have both at the same time. This is a very persuasive argument and involves a number of inter-related points. In this section, we deal with four of the main points supporting the argument that PR promotes instability. These are as follows:

1 PR produces coalition governments which are unstable by virtue of being made up of several parties, and therefore governments tend to change more often.
2 Coalition governments are not accountable, having been formed on the basis of backroom deals between party leaders after the election; the parties' manifesto promises are forgotten in the rush to gain power; the voters' wishes are ignored.
3 PR systems ensure the easy entry of small and extremist parties into parliament, threatening the stability of the government, particularly in those cases where the extremists hold the balance of power in the parliament.
4 PR systems are more complex than non-PR systems, adding an extra burden to the voters and raising the question of whether they really understand what is going on.

To counteract the first main area of criticism, to rigorously assess the stability of government in terms of how long it stays in office is fraught with difficulties (e.g. Laver and Schofield, 1991). What defines a change of government: an election, a new prime minister, a cabinet reshuffle? For instance, according to some definitions, the British Conservatives' replacement of Margaret Thatcher by John Major in 1990 constituted a change of government. Furthermore, allowance must be made for systems like Germany where it is difficult to unseat a government in mid-term or Switzerland where a government cannot be touched in mid-term.

Table 7.3 provides some indication of the variations in government longevity and their relation to coalition (see also Gallagher *et al.*, 1995: 327–8). As expected, with 94.7 per cent of its elections producing a legislative majority for one party, Britain lies on the more stable end of the spectrum. The significant point, however, is that it does not have the *most* stable record. It is equalled or surpassed by Austria, Iceland, Ireland, the Netherlands and Luxembourg, all of which use PR and have far less frequent single-party majorities in parliament. In other words, the evidence in Table 7.3 suggests that while FPTP helps to promote governmental longevity (and hence

Table 7.3   Parliamentary majorities and government stability, 1945–92

	Number of governments	Per cent of governments where one party controls legislative majority
France	53	1.9
Italy	51	0.0
Switzerland	47	0.0
Finland	39	25.6
Belgium	37	8.1
Denmark	27	0.0
Germany	24	0.0
Norway	23	26.1
Sweden	22	13.6
United Kingdom	19	94.7
Iceland	19	0.0
Ireland	19	36.8
Austria	18	5.6
Netherlands	17	0.0
Luxembourg	15	0.0

Source: Derived from Gallagher *et al.* (1995: Table 12.2).

'stability'), it is quite possible for PR systems to have the same result.

The second main area of criticism of coalition governments is that they are undemocratic. There are two parts to this argument. First, coalitions are produced after the election as a result of meetings in smoke-filled rooms between party leaders. The voters' 'word' on which party or parties should form the government is peripheral to the outcome; what matters is who can strike the better deal. As always it is easy to find examples of coalition governments being formed in this way, but equally there are examples of coalition bargains between parties being struck *before* the election, so voters know what they are voting for. For that matter, in systems where coalitions are the norm, voters may be well aware of the likely coalition arrangements that will emerge after the election. In short, the whole process of coalition formation can be entirely predictable: 'Thus we should not get too bewitched by an image of the political future of most European states being settled not by the electorate but by the wheeling and dealing of party leaders' (Gallagher *et al.*, 1995: 303). Furthermore, as Geoffrey K. Roberts (1975: 221) has noted: 'British experience in 1974 demonstrates that even the plurality system is no guarantee that post-election manoeuvres may not be required as a preliminary to the formation of a government.'

In addition, coalitions are said to be undemocratic because they make a mockery of manifesto pledges. At least in the case of single-party governments, a voter can hold the government to account if it does not fulfil campaign pledges. The evidence shows that, on the whole, British governments have a good record of implementing manifesto proposals (Rallings, 1987; Rose, 1980). To date, there have been no studies of the record of coalition governments elsewhere in Europe, and '[o]n the face of things we would expect a lower proportion of pledges to be honored in coalition systems, since different coalition partners may well make conflicting pledges on the same theme; thus one is inevitably bound to be broken' (Gallagher *et al.*, 1995: 347). Of course, such a situation need not arise wherever coalition arrangements are agreed before the election, allowing the partners to coordinate their policy proposals.

While FPTP may have a good record in producing safe legislative majorities and therefore in facilitating the implementation of manifesto promises, there is a question mark over the extent to which this is a sufficient indicator of government stability. For instance, the government may be stable because it has a majority of seats, but how *representative* is it? In other words, to what extent is it stable in terms of numbers of votes? The UK government elected in 1992 had the support of just 41.9 per cent of those who voted. By contrast, other governments elected around the same time were far more representative of public opinion, e.g. Austria (1990), 74.9 per cent; the Netherlands (1989), 67.2 per cent; Finland (1987), 58.8 per cent; Ireland (1992), 58.4 per cent; and Germany (1990), 54.8 per cent. Another aspect of 'stability' which is worth noting is the issue of continuity of government policies. The adversarial nature of British politics is characterized by sharp shifts in policy as governments change (Finer, 1975). By contrast, the more 'consensual' nature of coalitional systems – due to the need to strike deals between parties – ensures a far greater degree of policy consistency over time (Lijphart, 1984).

The third main area of criticism of proportional electoral systems is that, by making it easier for smaller parties to win seats in parliament, these systems facilitate the rise of extremist parties. This not only increases the risk of hung parliaments, with governments being hostage to the vagaries of extremist politicians, but it also

Table 7.4 **The electoral performance of the extreme Right in western Europe**

PR rank and country	Electoral system	1980s vote (%)	Parties competing in 1990s
1. Germany	list PR	—	Republicans
3. Netherlands	list PR	0.6	Center Democrats
8. Switzerland	list PR	3.2	Swiss Democrats
11. Italy	list PR	6.4	Italian Social Movement
14. Belgium	list PR	1.3	(Flemish Block), National Front
36. France	majoritarian	6.5	National Front

Note: See Table 7.1 for details on the PR rank.
Sources: Table 7.1; Gallagher *et al.* (1995: 200).

affects the stability of the political system by giving undue representation to politicians and parties whose views are abhorrent to the majority of citizens.

It may be the case that extremist parties are more commonly found in proportional systems, but how much of this is due to the fact that proportional systems are more common than non-proportional systems? Extremist parties can also achieve prominence in non-proportional systems, in particular wherever they can take advantage of a geographical concentration in their support base. As we see in Table 7.4 – taken from a recent comparative assessment of these new parties (Gallagher *et al.*, 1995) – five of the six prominent examples of the rise of extreme right parties have occurred in proportional systems; the sixth case is France, where Jean Marie Le Pen and his National Front have made shock waves in a majoritarian-based system. The other point worth remarking on in Table 7.4 is the lack of any apparent relationship between the degree of proportionality of the electoral system (as shown by the PR ranking) and the relative success of extreme right parties.

There is little doubt, however, that proportional systems can make life easier for extremist politicians and parties. One could always develop a defence of PR along the lines that, in a democracy, all views and opinions should have equal rights of expression and that, morally therefore, such parties should be facilitated, not blocked. One could even make the argument that, by allowing extremists into the parliament, the electoral system might be playing a moderating role, encouraging such parties to work within the system, rather than seeking to overthrow it.

Of course, such arguments may have a moral force, but they do not really answer the criticism that PR facilitates the entry of extremism. If the objective is to try to prevent extremist parties and politicians from being elected, then what can proportional systems do to meet it? In fact, there are two ways of meeting this objective, both of which are currently in use: one is to apply quota rules (see pp. 70–71), such as the German 5 per cent rule. This ensures that smaller parties are excluded from parliament, and, since extremist parties usually are smaller, this affects them. The second method is to pass a law banning certain categories of parties, as used in Germany to prevent the rise of neo-Nazi parties.

At this point, the critic of proportional electoral systems might raise the following set of objections: these legal blocks on parties are hardly cast-iron guarantees against the danger of extremists 'breaking through'; non-proportional systems provide a more effective, and simpler, means of achieving the same result; and, in any event, operating such legal restrictions is somewhat against the principle of proportionality and is, therefore, contradictory. Each of these points has some validity. The only counter to them is to remind ourselves that, to date, the entry of extremist parties has not exactly been a mad rush (as indicated by Table 7.4), and this places a question mark over the degree to which we need to be unduly concerned about them.

The final area of criticism of PR systems is that, because they are more complex, they are more likely to confuse voters. The voters may not be entirely certain of what their vote means and of how the final election result has been calculated. After all, it is far easier to understand how a politician has been elected because he or she had more votes than anyone else, than it is to make sense of how modified-Sainte-Laguë produced a certain number of seats for your preferred party. If the voters are more uncertain, more confused, then perhaps there is a greater likelihood of their being alienated by the complexities of the system.

One problem with such an argument is that it reveals a rather low expectation of voters. Why should they be more confused under PR systems? And, for that matter, why should it matter that the voters do not understand precisely how the final election result has been produced? Surely, the fact that the result is more proportional should have a higher priority than whether the complexities of the system are understood. Setting aside these objections, it is useful to examine the evidence of voter trends under different electoral systems. The issues of voter confusion and/or alienation could be said to manifest themselves in terms of greater numbers of invalid votes (also referred to as 'spoiled', or 'informal', votes) or in terms of lower voter turnout. Table 7.5 provides some indication of how these have varied across the different systems in recent years. Needless to say, invalid votes and low turnout can have many causes, such as the rise of anti-party sentiment generally or the fact that, in some systems (notably Switzerland and the USA), voters are called upon to vote too often. In some cases where laws are operating which require voters to turn out to vote (notably Australia, Belgium, Greece and Luxembourg), it is to be expected that the turnout figures are artificially inflated.

There are two points worth making about Table 7.5. First, there is little evidence to support the assumed negative relationship between the proportionality of the electoral system (which, in this instance, can be taken to mean its 'complexity') and numbers of invalid votes or size of turnout. Some of the most proportional systems have both high turnout and low numbers of invalid votes (e.g. Denmark, Germany and the Netherlands). In the case of turnout, if we take the twenty countries where turnout is not compulsory, Britain – with one of the simplest electoral systems – has one of the worst records of turnout; only seven countries have worse turnout figures in recent elections (Finland, France, Ireland, Japan, Portugal, Spain and Switzerland). This tallies with Lijphart's more comprehensive analysis (1994a: 6–7) which reveals that average voting participation is about nine percentage points higher in PR systems than in non-PR systems.

Second, for the most part, the percentages of invalid votes are hardly very significant. Indeed, with the exception of Italy (5.9 per cent), in none of the cases where there is voluntary turnout, does the percentage rise above 1.6 per cent. (The Italian case is somewhat unusual in that, while there is no compulsory voting law as such, there is a practice of recording the names of those people who have not voted.) We would expect higher proportions of invalid votes in compulsory turnout systems where voters are forced to vote against their will (e.g. McAllister and Makkai, 1993), and this is demonstrated in Table 7.5 where invalid votes range between 4.6–6.1 per cent.

Table 7.5 Invalid votes and voter turnout under different electoral systems

Country	Election	Invalid votes (%)	Turnout (%)	PR ranking[a]
Belgium	1987	6.1	93.4*	14
Italy	1987	5.9	90.5	11
Luxembourg	1989	4.8	87.3*	13
Australia	1987	4.6	93.8*	30
Greece	1989	1.9	84.5*	21
Austria	1986	1.6	90.5	4
Portugal	1987	1.6	72.6	23
Japan	1986	1.5	71.4	27
Spain	1986	1.4	70.6	31
France	1988	1.3	66.2	36
Sweden	1988	1.1	86.0	6
Iceland	1987	1.0	90.1	25
Germany	1987	0.8	84.3	1
Ireland	1989	0.8	68.5	15
Israel	1988	0.8	79.7	10
Canada	1988	0.6	75.5	35
Denmark	1988	0.6	85.7	7
Malta	1987	0.6	96.1	20
New Zealand	1987	0.5	87.2	33
Finland	1987	0.4	72.1	12
Netherlands	1986	0.3	85.8	3
Norway	1985	0.1	84.0	19
UK	1987	0.1	75.4	32
Switzerland	1987	0.0	46.1	8

Notes: [a] For details on PR ranking, see Table 7.1.
* Countries operating compulsory voting rules.
The countries have been ranked in terms of percentage of invalid votes.
Sources: Table 7.1; Mackie and Rose (1991).

In sum, the evidence of a trade-off between the proportionality of an electoral system and measures of governmental or system stability is, for the most part, conspicuous by its absence. On the contrary, it would seem more accurate to conclude from this discussion that, if anything, proportional electoral systems are associated with greater degrees of stability. Indeed, in his comprehensive analysis of the post-war records of different systems in terms of the performance and effectiveness of democracy, Arend Lijphart concludes (1994a: 8):

the conventional wisdom is wrong in positing a trade-off between the advantages of plurality and PR systems. The superior performance of

PR with regard to political representation is not counterbalanced by an inferior record on governmental effectiveness; if anything, the record of the PR countries on macro-economic management appears to be a bit better than that of the plurality systems – but not to the extent that the differences are statistically significant. The practical conclusion is that PR is to be preferred over plurality since it offers both better representation and at least as effective public policy-making.

7.5 The strategic effects of electoral systems

In some senses, the debate on the proportionality and party system effects of electoral systems is generally complete; it is difficult to see what there is left to say about these issues. Accordingly, in recent years, attention has started to shift to other aspects of possible electoral system influence. It could be argued that all the issues dealt with in the previous sections share in common a concern with the macro-level effects of electoral systems, in terms of how they influence the electoral process in a global sense. An alternative perspective is to assess the micro-level effects of electoral systems. Here the concern is less with the *electoral* effects of electoral systems and more with their *strategic* effects. Specifically, it can be expected that both the politicians and the voters will operate differently under different electoral systems. We begin with the politicians.

In order to assess the strategic effects of electoral systems on politicians it is useful to draw a distinction between *party-based* and *candidate-based* electoral systems: the former personified by closed list systems like Spain (see pp. 72–74 above), the latter including FPTP, STV and open list systems. In essence, this relates to one aspect of ballot structure which has not so far been considered, namely the degree of electoral choice it facilitates; the scope for voters to choose between different candidates. It is not just the question of whether the ballot structure is categoric or ordinal; also relevant is the degree of ordinality of the system, or the degree of 'intra-party electoral choice' it facilitates (Katz, 1980). Where the system allows high levels of intra-party choice (as best represented by STV), there is a tendency for parties to campaign in a decentralized fashion; there is more emphasis on the campaigns of individual candidates and, on occasion, this can result in faction-fighting between candidates. In short, then, there are significant differences in the nature of a party's campaign depending on the electoral system (Katz, 1980).

This issue can be taken a stage further to assess the nature of parliamentary representation. In chapter 1, a distinction was drawn between the 'principal-agent' and 'microcosm' conceptions of representation, the former supported by opponents of PR, the latter by its proponents. This debate is focusing specifically on the question of representation in the *aggregate*, in terms of the collective assembly of parliament. An alternative perspective is to focus on the representative role of *individual* MPs. In his famous address to the voters of Bristol in 1774, Edmund Burke set out two competing concepts of the role of the representative in his or her constituency: as a *delegate* of the voters or a *trustee*. According to the first type, the MP is said to listen closely to the views of the voters. There are even suggestions that he or she is 'mandated' by the voters to take certain decisions. According to the second type, in the trustee role – favoured by Burke – the MP is elected to act on the behalf of the constituency as a whole. He or she is better placed than anyone to weigh up the often conflicting views of his or her voters, and come to a considered decision, without needing to always check back with the voters.

In party-based electoral systems, where the voter is choosing between parties and not candidates, there is little scope for mandating the politicians (apart, that is, from the mandate given to the parties), and therefore we can expect a greater tendency for politicians to act as trustees. Indeed, in such systems, the principal 'voting-constituency' of the individual politician is not the voters, but rather the 'selectorates' who determine whether he or she will appear on the list, and in which rank position. By contrast, in candidate-based electoral systems, where the MPs are clamouring for precious personal votes (in some cases, such as under STV, in direct competition with fellow party candidates), we can expect a greater tendency for MPs to act as delegates.

Evidence in support of this argument is provided by a survey of the activities of Members of the European Parliament (MEPs). Given that there is a large range of different electoral systems used to elect the MEPs, the European Parliament provides a useful laboratory to test the influence of electoral systems on parliamentary representation. This study found that MEPs elected under candidate-based electoral systems – and particularly systems which were constituency-based (namely the UK and Ireland) – were more inclined to have regular contact with individual voters. By contrast, the MEPs elected under party-based systems were prone to have closer links with organized interests. The study concluded that 'individual voters are better – or at least more frequently – served by representatives elected under district based systems and where voters can choose candidates' (Bowler and Farrell, 1993: 64).

Ballot structure can also have an effect on the strategic calculations of voters. In a system where voters can make only a single, categoric decision on which candidate (in the case of FPTP), or party (in the case of closed PR list) to support, the voting exercise is relatively straightforward. The voter selects the appropriate candidate or party and votes accordingly. There is some limited scope for strategic voting under the FPTP electoral system. Take the scenario of a voter who likes a particular candidate but knows full well that this candidate does not stand a chance of being elected. This could be a situation where the candidate in question is expected to come in a bad third in the constituency race. The voter has one of three options: to vote for the candidate anyway despite the fact that this vote will be wasted; not to bother voting, or to vote for the candidate expected to come second, on the grounds that *anyone* would be better than the sitting MP. This last option opens up the possibility of what is referred to as 'tactical voting'. Survey evidence reveals that in the UK an increasing number of voters stuck in 'safe' seats have been making use of this option. According to the analysis of Niemi *et al.* (1992; 1993), the level of tactical voting had risen to about one in six voters in 1987. This figure has been disputed by Evans and Heath (1993), who put the level of tactical voting at closer to 6 per cent. According to subsequent analysis of the 1992 election by Evans (1994), tactical voting was found to have increased to 9 per cent, suggesting that even when using a more conservative measure, the phenomenon does appear to be on the increase.

The scope for strategic voting increases once we start to complicate the electoral process and, in particular, when we take account of more complex electoral systems. For instance, where there are different levels of election occurring at the same time, the voter can take advantage of this situation and vary his or her support for the different parties. This phenomenon of 'split-ticket' voting, or 'ticket-splitting', is particularly acute in the USA where voters increasingly split their votes between the Republicans and the Democrats, providing one indicator of the extent to which American parties are 'in decline'. According to Martin P. Wattenberg (1994: 23), '[t]icket-splitting has assumed massive proportions compared to the rate just two decades ago, and only a small minority of the electorate now believes that one should vote strictly on the basis of party labels'. Split-ticket voting can be expected wherever there are two or more levels of election coinciding (e.g. on the Australian case, see Bowler and Denemark, 1993). It is also a feature of the two-vote system. As the evidence presented in chapter 5 revealed (see Table 5.3), over the years the German Free Democrats have successfully exploited split-ticket voting to cushion themselves against the danger of falling below the 5 per cent threshold.

There are clear limits to the strategic options available to voters in the systems discussed so far. What is unique about preferential electoral systems – such as the alternative vote, STV and certain types of open list system – is that they provide such large scope for voters to express more complex and nuanced preferences. Voters can switch and change between one candidate and another at will (and, in STV, between one party and another). There is plenty of scope to retain loyalty for the Conservative Party, for example, while, at the same time, giving a preference to a Green candidate whose policies appear attractive. In short, then, under preferential electoral systems (characterized by an ordinal ballot structure) there is great scope for voters to act strategically (Bowler, 1996; Bowler and Farrell, 1996). As we saw in chapter 6, there is plenty of evidence from the Irish case over the years that voters have made use of their vote transfers strategically, for instance, to influence the possible formation of a coalition government (see pp. 124–26).

7.6 The politics of electoral reform: a multitude of preferences

Given the plethora of different electoral systems in operation through-out the world, it is difficult to escape from the conclusion that each one is ultimately the product of particular national circumstances and actors. Despite the best efforts of learned electoral system specialists to offer kindly words of advice to 'electoral engineers' on specific features of existing electoral systems that might warrant incorporation (Lijphart, 1994; Taagepera and Shugart, 1989; Sartori, 1995), it is difficult to disagree with Pippa Norris's (1995a: 4) observation that 'electoral systems are rarely designed, they are born kicking and screaming into the world out of a messy, incremental compromise between contending factions battling for survival, determined by power politics'.

Given the 'messy' nature of electoral reform, what causes countries with long-established electoral systems to opt for reform? Up until relatively recently, with the exceptions of countries like France or Argentina, the bias was very much in favour of keeping the existing electoral system regardless of its faults. The abiding principle was: '[f]amiliarity breeds stability' (Taagepera and Shugart, 1989: 218). Dunleavy and Margetts (1995: 11) suggest that such a view reflected an 'orthodoxy' in the literature favouring the *status quo*: '[s]een against this type of argument, 1993–94 appears as an *annus mirabilis* in which three established liberal democracies – Italy, Japan, and New Zealand – radically changed their voting systems'.

It is difficult to establish exactly what has caused electoral reform to become so high on the agenda of politics. In a review of the debates in Israel, Italy, Japan, New Zealand and the UK, Pippa Norris (1995a: 7) discerns three long-term factors which these countries (or some combination of them) share in common and which, at least in part, appear to have played a role in triggering demands for electoral reform: (1) electoral change (and, in particular, the weakening of electoral alignments); (2) 'political scandals and/or government failures which rock public confidence in the political system'; and (3) the ability of voters (in Italy and New Zealand) to use referendums to force the hands of politicians. Norris comments: 'Long-term conditions created the potential for change, and electoral reform is seen as completing a process of democratization which would put an end to deep-rooted failures in the political system.'

Dunleavy and Margetts (1995) distinguish between 'plurality rule' countries and PR countries, and they suggest that the specific motivations for change have been influenced by the nature of the existing electoral system in each case. In the case of plurality countries, the process of electoral change – and, specifically, the rise of new parties – increased the disproportional tendencies of the electoral system, as well as the amount of attention to these disproportional tendencies. As has been discussed in chapter 2, the FPTP system can operate quite proportionally in a two-party system, such as the USA, but as the system becomes more fragmented (e.g. as shown by the increased vote of the Liberals/Liberal Democrats in the UK), the inherent disproportional tendencies of the electoral system become evident.

In PR countries, the push for electoral reform has had different root causes. Here, by definition, there is less concern about the proportionality of the system. According to Dunleavy and Margetts (1995), there is, instead, a concern about questions of accountability and parliamentary representation, relating either to the large electoral districts in PR list systems or to the degree of party control over the candidate lists. They refer to four cases: Italy, Japan, Israel and the Netherlands. While in general this is a credible argument, one can take issue with certain aspects of detail. For instance, the (now defunct) Japanese single non-transferable vote system could hardly be categorized as 'proportional' (Shiratori, 1995), and the catalyst for change in Italy and Japan had rather more to do with issues of political corruption generally than with the specifics of parliamentary accountability.

Electoral reform is now a much more realistic proposition than a decade ago. Some countries have changed their system and others (the UK included) are considering it. It is, therefore, both relevant and important to complete our examination of the different electoral systems with a brief assessment on whether we can decide on which is best. There is some disagreement on this issue among the specialists on electoral systems. They tend to break down into two main camps: those who suggest that the aim should be for 'simple' electoral systems, and those who tend to favour more complex electoral systems.

In the first camp, for instance, there is Giovanni Sartori (1995) who favours the (French) second ballot system. Blais and Massicotte (1996) also express a preference for majoritarian systems. In both cases the argument in favour of majoritarian systems revolves around the importance of government stability. There is also the idea that when choosing between electoral systems, a guiding principle should be 'simple is best'. While agreeing with this principle, Taagepera and Shugart (1989: 236) tend, however, to hedge their bets, stating that they have 'no emotional attachment to any electoral system'. Their starting point is that electoral systems are best left alone: '[k]eeping the ills we know of may be better than leaping into the unknown'. However, in the circumstances of adopting electoral rules in a newly democratizing country, Taagepera and Shugart (1989: 236) indicate a preference for small, multi-member constituencies, with some kind of proportional electoral formula. They also stress the need to keep it simple: there should be 'no complexities such as adjustment seats, thresholds, multi-stage elections, or multi-tiered seat allocations'. Ultimately, in the closing sentence of their book they express a guarded preference for STV.

In the second camp, Arend Lijphart shows no apparent concern about the complexity of certain electoral systems. In his advice to would-be electoral reformers, he stresses the virtues of such features as two-tier districting, national legal thresholds, vote transferability and *apparentement* (Lijphart, 1994: 145). While Lijphart does tend to agree with Taagepera and Shugart that in the case of existing electoral systems the preference should be for 'incremental improvements, not revolutionary upheaval' (ibid.: 151), his advice for 'electoral engineers in the new democracies' is to examine 'all the options' (ibid.: 152). Dunleavy and Margetts are even more explicit in making a virtue of electoral system complexity. They suggest that the reforms of the early 1990s (in Italy, Japan and New Zealand) reflect an 'apparent convergence of liberal democracies' (Dunleavy and Margetts, 1995: 26) towards what they call 'mixed' electoral systems (referred to in chapter 5 above as the two-vote system). Contrary to Sartori's (1994: 75) dismissal of the two-vote system as 'a bastard-producing hybrid', Dunleavy and Margetts (1995: 27) are inclined to see it in a much more positive light: 'It combines the accountability strengths of plurality rule in single-member constituencies with the offsetting proportional qualities of regional or national lists.'

Even in this short review, we can see that there is little agreement between the various specialists: Blais and Massicotte and Sartori favour majoritarian systems (and especially the second ballot system); Taagepera and Shugart reveal a sympathy for STV; Lijphart appears to favour list systems with two-tier districting; Dunleavy and Margetts see a 'convergence' towards the two-vote system. If the specialists cannot agree on which is best, it is hardly surprising that the politicians have come up with such a wide range of different electoral systems.

7.7 Conclusion

The study of electoral systems can reveal a lot about political behaviour. The proportionality of the system plays a significant role in deciding who wins and who loses in the election game, on the constellation of parties in parliament (and therefore also in government), and on the characteristics of the individual MPs. In turn, this raises questions relating to the degree of stability of the government and political system, though, as we have seen, the evidence in support of the argument that proportionality produces instability is tenuous. In this respect, then, we have a conclusion which favours proportional electoral systems because apparently we can have both! We can have a proportional electoral system and, at the same time, a stable political system.

Is it possible to be more specific about which proportional system is preferable? Apart from the issue of proportionality and its consequences, we have seen how electoral systems can have other effects, in terms of the nature of parliamentary representation, styles of election campaigning by parties and candidates, and the strategic actions of voters on polling day. It is clear that candidate-based electoral systems, and particularly those which facilitate preferential voting, provide greater scope for voters to act strategically when voting; they also help to tie the politicians into a closer relationship with their voters, encouraging closer attention to constituency work. In short, what this amounts to is a suggestion that, of all the existing systems considered in this book, the STV system perhaps comes closest to an ideal electoral system. It combines the virtues of proportionality with those of preferential voting. It is a system which politicians, given a choice, would probably least like to see introduced, but which voters, given a choice, should choose.

Notes

[1] The Least-squares index is calculated as follows: square the vote–seat differences for each party (ignoring 'others' – usually parties with less than 0.5 per cent of the vote); sum them; divide the total by two; and then take the square root (Gallagher, 1991; Lijphart, 1994: 60–1). The principal advantage of this index over the others is that it is not so easily distorted by the presence of small parties (a particular problem with the Rae index), nor has it too many problems with systems containing large numbers of parties (a particular problem with the Loosemore-Hanby index).

[2] The index of 'effective' number of parliamentary parties is calculated as follows: 1 divided by the sum of the squared percentage seats for each party.

GLOSSARY

Note: Cross-entries are emboldened.

Apparentement

To get around the problem for smaller parties of 'wasted' votes in list systems – i.e. where they just fail to win seats – two or more parties may opt to formally link their lists, contesting the election as an alliance and thereby increasing the prospect of having candidates elected. *Apparentement* is used most commonly in **d'Hondt** systems to compensate for the relatively low disproportionality of the result (compared with other list systems).

Ballot structure

The nature and degree of choice available to the voter in an election. The basic distinction is between a categoric ballot structure (such as under first past the post (FPTP) and certain list systems) where the voter can declare a preference for just one candidate (or party), and an ordinal ballot structure (such as under preferential electoral systems and some list systems) where, to varying degrees, the voter can rank-order candidates in order of preference.

Cube rule

This suggests that the FPTP electoral system has a built-in mechanism to produce single-party parliamentary majorities, and thereby ensure 'strong' and stable governments. It can be formalized as follows: if the ratio of votes that two parties receive is A : B, then this will result in the following ratio of seats, $A^3:B^3$. In other words, the party which receives the most votes wins an inflated majority of seats in parliament. Recent evidence indicates that this rule no longer applies in the UK.

d'Hondt

Named after Victor d'Hondt, and referred to in the USA as the Jefferson method, this is the most common divisor used in the **highest average** system, and (together with **largest remainder** Imperiali) is regarded as one of the least proportional of the list systems. It operates with the following divisors: 1, 2, 3, 4, etc.

District magnitude

Literally the size of the constituency in terms of numbers of MPs (e.g. a single-seat constituency has a district magnitude (DM) of one). Generally the FPTP and majoritarian electoral systems have a DM of one, while the proportional systems have DMs greater than one. The size of the DM has a very important bearing on the overall proportionality of a proportional representation (PR) system: the larger the DM the more proportional the system.

Droop quota

Named after H. R. Droop, and often referred to as the Hagenbach-Bischoff quota, this is used in **largest remainder** list systems and in the single transferable vote (STV) electoral system to determine the allocation of seats. It is regarded as less proportional than **Hare**, but more proportional than **Imperiali**. It is calculated as follows: first, the total valid vote is divided by one plus the number of seats and then one is added to the total (ignoring decimal points).

Electoral formula

The counting rules which apply in a given electoral system. This is generally the way in which one distinguishes between the different electoral systems, such as: FPTP (where a candidate requires a plurality of votes to be elected), majoritarian systems (where a candidate requires an overall majority), STV (where the **Droop** quota is used to determine how many votes a candidate requires), and the list systems (which separate, in turn, into **largest remainder** and **highest average** systems). The electoral formula has an important bearing on overall proportionality (though not as important as **district magnitude**).

Electoral law

The family of rules governing the process of elections: from the calling of the election, through the stages of candidate nomination, party campaigning and voting, and right up to the stage of counting votes and determining the actual election result.

Electoral system

One part of the **electoral law** which specifically deals with the final determination of who is elected. Electoral systems determine the means by which votes are translated into seats in the process of electing politicians into office.

Gerrymandering

The practice of redrawing constituency boundaries with the intention of producing an inflated number of seats for a party, usually the governing party. Named after Governor Gerry of Massachusetts in 1812 who produced a constituency boundary which resembled a salamander, giving rise to the term 'gerrymander'.

Hare quota

Named after Thomas Hare (who devised the STV electoral system) and often referred to as the 'simple quota', this is the most common quota used in the **largest remainder** system to determine the allocation of seats, and tends to produce highly proportional results. It is calculated as follows: total valid vote divided by the number of seats.

Highest average

This is one of the **electoral formulae** used by list systems to arrange the translation of votes into seats, and is far more common than the alternative, the **largest remainder** system. It operates by use of divisors, of which there are two main forms in use: **d'Hondt** (by far the most common) and **modified Sainte-Laguë**. Each party's votes are divided by a series of divisors to produce an average vote. The party with the 'highest average' vote after each stage of the process wins a seat, and its vote is then divided by the next divisor. The process continues until all the seats have been filled.

Imperiali quota

Used in Italy until 1993, this is regarded as the least proportional of the **largest remainder** systems. It is calculated as follows: total valid vote divided by two plus the number of seats.

Largest remainder

Referred to in the USA as the Hamilton method. This is one of the **electoral formulae** used by list systems to arrange the translation of votes into seats (the other is **highest average**). It operates by use of an electoral quota, the most common of which are **Hare**, **Droop** and **Imperiali**. The counting process is in two stages: (1) those parties with votes exceeding the quota are awarded seats, and the quota is subtracted from their total vote; (2) those parties left with the greatest number of votes (the 'largest remainder') are awarded the remaining seats in order of vote size.

Malapportionment

A situation in which there are imbalances in the population densities of constituencies which favour some parties over others (e.g. such as happens when constituency boundaries are not redrawn to take account of rural depopulation).

Modified Sainte-Laguë

Named after A. Sainte-Laguë, and associated most with Scandinavian countries, this **highest average** divisor tends to produce more proportional results than the more common **d'Hondt** divisor. It operates with the following divisors: 1.4, 3, 5, 7, etc. The 1.4 divisor was brought in to reduce the overall proportionality of the original pure Sainte-Laguë system which was seen as too proportional. Referred to in the USA as the Webster method, pure Sainte-Laguë uses the following divisors: 1, 3, 5, 7. It was adopted by New Zealand in 1993.

Monotonicity

If a candidate's vote increases this should improve the prospects of winning a seat. As pointed out in the formal literature on voting theory, it is possible under preferential electoral systems (such as alternative vote or STV) for a candidate's prospects to be hindered, not helped, by an increase in first preference votes. This potential for a non-monotonic result is seen by some as a flaw of preferential electoral systems; others point out that it is difficult to find examples of it ever actually occurring.

Panachage

This is the most 'open' form of **ballot structure** available in list systems, and is operated in Luxembourg and Switzerland. The ballot paper allows voters to give preferences to candidates from more than one party.

Two-tier districting

Most of the list systems carve up a country into regions or constituencies, thereby reducing the size of the **district magnitude** and, therefore, the overall proportionality of the result. To help increase proportionality, a certain number of seats are allocated in a second-tier such as across the nation as a whole. All remaining votes from the first-tier which have not been used to fill seats are pooled and the distribution of the remaining seats is determined in the second-tier.

Überhangmandate *seats*

Literally surplus mandates or bonus seats. In the German version of the two-vote electoral system where the number of constituency seats a party wins is subtracted from the number of list seats it is being allocated, it is possible for a party to win more constituency seats in one *Land* (or state) than the total to which its share of the vote would entitle it. Whenever this happens the party is allowed to retain these extra seats and the size of the Bundestag is temporarily enlarged.

BIBLIOGRAPHY

Allard, Crispin (1995), 'Lack of Monotonicity – Revisited', *Representation* 33: 48–50.

Amy, Douglas J. (1993), *Real Choices, New Voices: The Case for Proportional Representation Elections in the United States*, New York: Columbia University Press.

Andeweg, Rudy B. and Galen A. Irwin (1993), *Dutch Government and Politics*, Basingstoke: Macmillan.

Australian Electoral Commission (1993), *Election Statistics, 1993: Full Distribution of Preferences, House of Representatives*, Canberra: Australian Government Publishing Service.

Bax, Mart (1976), *Harpstrings and Confessions*, Assen: Van Gorcum.

Bean, Clive, Ian McAllister and John Warhurst (1990), *The Greening of Australian Politics: The 1990 Federal Election*, Melbourne: Longman Cheshire.

Belin, Laura (1996), 'An Array of Mini-Parties Wage Futile Parliamentary Campaigns', *Transition* 23 February: 15–19.

Blackburn, Robert (1995), *The Electoral System in Britain*, Basingstoke: Macmillan.

Blais, André and R. K. Carty (1991), 'The Psychological Impact of Electoral Laws: Measuring Duverger's Elusive Factor', *British Journal of Political Science* 21: 79–93.

Blais, André and Louis Massicotte (1996), 'Electoral Systems', in Lawrence LeDuc, Richard G. Niemi and Pippa Norris (eds), *Comparing Democracies*, Thousand Oaks, CA: Sage.

Blondel, Jean (1969), *An Introduction to Comparative Government*, London: Weidenfeld and Nicolson.

Bogdanor, Vernon (1981), *The People and the Party System: The Referendum and Electoral Reform in British Politics*, Cambridge: Cambridge University Press.

Bogdanor, Vernon (1984), *What is Proportional Representation? A Guide to the Issues*, Oxford: Martin Robertson.

Bogdanor, Vernon (ed.) (1985), *Representatives of the People?*, Aldershot: Gower.

Bogdanor, Vernon and David Butler (eds) (1983), *Democracy and Elections: Electoral Systems and Their Political Consequences*, Cambridge: Cambridge University Press.

Boll, Bernhard and Thomas Poguntke (1992), 'Germany: The 1990 All-German Election Campaign', in Shaun Bowler and David Farrell (eds), *Electoral Strategies and Political Marketing*, Basingstoke: Macmillan.

Bowler, Shaun (1996), 'Reasoning Voters, Voter Behaviour and Institutions', in David Farrell, David Broughton, David Denver and Justin Fisher (eds), *British Elections and Parties Yearbook, 1996*, London: Frank Cass.

Bowler, Shaun and David Denemark (1993), 'Split Ticket Voting in Australia: Dealignment and Inconsistent Votes Reconsidered', *Australian Journal of Political Science* 28: 19–37.

Bowler, Shaun and David Farrell (1993), 'Legislator Shirking and Voter Monitoring: Impacts of European Parliament Electoral Systems upon Legislator–Voter Relationships', *Journal of Common Market Studies* 31: 45–69.

Bowler, Shaun and David Farrell (1994), 'A British PR Election: Testing STV with London's Voters', *Representation* 32: 90–5.

Bowler, Shaun and David Farrell (1996), 'Voter Strategies under Preferential Electoral Systems: A Single Transferable Vote Mock Ballot Survey of London Voters', in Colin Rallings, David Farrell, David Broughton and David Denver (eds), *British Elections and Parties Yearbook, 1995*, London: Frank Cass.

Bradley, Patrick (1995), 'STV and Monotonicity: A Hands-On Assessment', *Representation*, 33: 46–7.

Brams, Steven J. and Peter C. Fishburn (1984), 'Some Logical Defects of the Single Transferable Vote', in Arend Lijphart and Bernard Grofman (eds), *Choosing an Electoral System: Issues and Alternatives*, New York: Praeger.

Butler, David (1963), *The Electoral System in Britain Since 1918* (2nd edn), Oxford: Clarendon Press.

Butler, David (1983), 'Variants of the Westminster Model', in Vernon Bogdanor and David Butler (eds), *Democracy and Elections: Electoral Systems and Their Political Consequences*, Cambridge: Cambridge University Press.

Cain, Bruce, John Ferejohn and Morris Fiorina (1987), *The Personal Vote: Constituency Service and Electoral Independence*, Cambridge, MA: Harvard University Press.

Carstairs, Andrew McLaren (1980), *A Short History of Electoral Systems in Western Europe*, London: George, Allen and Unwin.

Carty, R. K. (1981), *Party and Parish Pump: Electoral Politics in Ireland*, Waterloo: Wilfrid Laurier University Press.

Chubb, Basil (1982), *The Government and Politics of Ireland* (2nd edn), London: Longman.

Cole, Alistair and Peter Campbell (1989), *French Electoral Systems and Elections since 1789*, Aldershot: Gower.

Cole, Philip (1995), 'Bonus Seats in the German Electoral System', *Representation* 33: 9–10.

Curtice, John (1992), 'The Hidden Surprise: The British Electoral System in 1992', *Parliamentary Affairs* 45: 466–74.

Curtice, John and Michael Steed (1982), 'Electoral Choice and the Production of Government: The Changing Operation of the Electoral System in the United Kingdom Since 1955', *British Journal of Political Science* 12: 249–98.

Darcy, Robert and Ian McAllister (1990), 'Ballot Position Effects', *Electoral Studies* 9: 5–17.

Darcy, Robert and Malcolm Mackerras (1993), 'Rotation of Ballots: Minimizing the Number of Rotations', *Electoral Studies* 12: 77–82.

Darcy, Robert, Susan Welch and Janet Clark (1994), *Women, Elections and Representation*, (2nd edn), Lincoln, NB: University of Nebraska Press.

Denver, David (1994), *Elections and Voting Behaviour in Britain*, (2nd edn), Hemel Hempstead: Harvester Wheatsheaf.

Denver, David and Gordon Hands (1989), 'Voter Reactions to a Preferential Ballot: Some Survey Evidence', *Politics* 9: 23–7.

De Winter, Lieven (1988), 'Belgium: Democracy or Oligarchy?', in Michael Gallagher and Michael Marsh (eds), *Candidate Selection in Comparative Perspective: The Secret Garden of Politics*, London: Sage.

Donovan, Mark (1995), 'The Politics of Electoral Reform in Italy', *International Political Science Review* 16: 47–64.

Dummett, Michael (1992), 'Towards a More Representative Voting System: The Plant Report', *New Left Review* 194: 98–113.

Dunleavy, Patrick (1991), 'Democracy in Britain: A Health Check for the 1990s', in Ivor Crewe, Pippa Norris, David Denver and David Broughton (eds), *British Elections and Parties Yearbook, 1991*, Hemel Hempstead: Harvester Wheatsheaf.

Dunleavy, Patrick and Helen Margetts (1995), 'Understanding the Dynamics of Electoral Reform', *International Political Science Review* 16: 9–29.

Dunleavy, Patrick, Helen Margetts and Stuart Weir (1992), 'Replaying the 1992 General Election: How Britain Would Have Voted under Alternative Electoral Systems', *LSE Public Policy Paper*, No. 3.

Dunleavy, Patrick, Helen Margetts and Stuart Weir (1993), 'The 1992 Election and the Legitimacy of British Democracy', in David Denver, Pippa Norris, David Broughton and Colin Rallings (eds), *British Elections and Parties Yearbook 1993*, Hemel Hempstead: Harvester Wheatsheaf.

Duverger, Maurice (1954), *Political Parties: Their Organization and Activity in the Modern State*, London: Methuen.

Duverger, Maurice (1986), 'Duverger's Law: Forty Years Later', in Bernard Grofman and Arend Lijphart (eds), *Electoral Laws and Their Political Consequences*, New York: Agathon Press.

Erickson, Lynda (1995), 'The October 1993 Election and the Canadian Party System', *Party Politics* 1: 133–44.

Evans, Geoffrey (1994), 'Tactical Voting and Labour's Prospects', in

Anthony Heath, Roger Jowell, John Curtice, with Bridget Taylor (eds), *Labour's Last Chance? The 1992 Election and Beyond*, Aldershot: Dartmouth.

Evans, Geoffrey and Anthony Heath (1993), 'A Tactical Error in the Analysis of Tactical Voting: A Response to Niemi, Whitten and Franklin', *British Journal of Political Science* 23: 131–7.

Farrell, Brian (1985), 'Ireland: From Friends and Neighbours to Clients and Partisans', in Vernon Bogdanor (ed.), *Representatives of the People?*, Aldershot: Gower.

Farrell, Brian (1988), 'Ireland', in Jean Blondel and Ferdinand Müller-Rommel (eds), *Cabinets in Western Europe*, Basingstoke: Macmillan.

Farrell, David (1994), 'Ireland: Centralization, Professionalization and Campaign Pressures', in Richard Katz and Peter Mair (eds), *How Parties Organize: Adaptation and Change in Party Organizations in Western Democracies*, London: Sage.

Farrell, David (1996), 'Ireland: A Party System Transformed?', in David Broughton and Mark Donovan (eds), *Changing Party Systems in Western Europe*, London: Pinter.

Farrell, David and Ian McAllister (1995), 'Legislative Recruitment to Upper Houses: The Australian Senate and House of Representatives Compared', *Journal of Legislative Studies* 1: 243–63.

Farrell, David, Ian McAllister and David Broughton (1994), 'The Changing British Voter Revisited: Patterns of Election Campaign Volatility Since 1964', in David Broughton, David Farrell, David Denver and Colin Rallings (eds), *British Elections and Parties Yearbook, 1994*, London: Frank Cass.

Farrell, David, Malcolm Mackerras and Ian McAllister (1996), 'What is STV? Single Transferable Vote Electoral Systems in Liberal Democracies', *Political Studies* 44: 24–43.

Finer, S E (ed.) (1975), *Adversary Politics and Electoral Reform*, London: Anthony Wigram.

Franklin, Mark and Philip Norton (eds) (1993), *Parliamentary Questions*, Oxford: Clarendon Press.

Gallagher, Michael (1975), 'Disproportionality in a Proportional Representation System: The Irish Experience', *Political Studies* 23: 501–13.

Gallagher, Michael (1978), 'Party Solidarity, Exclusivity and Inter-party Relationships in Ireland 1922–1977: The Evidence of Transfers', *Economic and Social Review* 10: 1–22.

Gallagher, Michael (1987), 'Does Ireland Need a New Electoral System?', *Irish Political Studies* 2: 27–48.

Gallagher, Michael (1990), 'The Election Results and the New Dáil', in Michael Gallagher and Richard Sinnott (eds), *How Ireland Voted 1989*, Galway: Centre for the Study of Irish Elections/PSAI Press.

Gallagher, Michael (1991), 'Proportionality, Disproportionality and Electoral Systems', *Electoral Studies* 10(1): 33–51.

Gallagher, Michael (1993), 'The Election of the 27th Dáil', in Michael Gallagher and Michael Laver (eds), *How Ireland Voted 1992*, Dublin: Folens/PSAI Press.

Gallagher, Michael and A. R. Unwin (1986), 'Electoral Distortion under STV Random Sampling Procedures', *British Journal of Political Science* 16: 243–68.

Gallagher, Michael, Michael Laver and Peter Mair (1995), *Representative Government in Modern Europe* (2nd edn), New York: McGraw-Hill.

Gladdish, Ken (1991), *Governing From the Centre: Politics and Policy-Making in the Netherlands*, London: Hurst and Company.

Goldey, David B. (1993), 'The French General Election of 21–28 March 1993', *Electoral Studies* 12: 291–314.

Grofman, Bernard and Arend Lijphart (eds) (1986), *Electoral Laws and Their Political Consequences*, New York: Agathon Press.

Hand, Geoffrey, Jacques Georgel and Christoph Sasse (eds) (1979), *European Electoral Systems Handbook*, London: Butterworths.

Harris, Paul (1992), 'Changing New Zealand's Electoral System: The 1992 Referendum', *Representation* 31(115): 53–7.

Harris, Paul (1993), 'Electoral Reform in New Zealand', *Representation* 32(117): 7–10.

Hart, Jennifer (1992), *Proportional Representation: Critics of the British Electoral System, 1820–1945*, Oxford: Clarendon Press.

Hermens, Ferdinand A. (1984), 'Representation and Proportional Representation', in Arend Lijphart and Bernard Grofman (eds), *Choosing an Electoral System: Issues and Alternatives*, New York: Praeger.

Hirczy, Wolfgang (1995), 'STV and the Representation of Women', *PS: Political Science and Politics* 28: 711–13.

Holliday, Ian (1994), 'Dealing in Green Votes: France, 1993', *Government and Opposition* 29(1): 64–79.

Irvine, William F. (1979), *Does Canada Need a New Electoral System?*, Kingston, Ontario: Institute of Intergovernmental Relations, Queen's University.

Jesse, Eckhard (1988), 'Split-voting in the Federal Republic of Germany: An Analysis of the Federal Elections from 1953 to 1987', *Electoral Studies* 7: 109–24.

Johnston, Ron (1986), 'Constituency Redistribution in Britain: Recent Issues', in Bernard Grofman and Arend Lijphart (eds), *Electoral Laws and their Political Consequences*, New York: Agathon Press.

Katz, Richard S. (1980), *A Theory of Parties and Electoral Systems*, Baltimore, MD: Johns Hopkins University Press.

Katz, Richard S. (1984), 'The Single Transferable Vote and Proportional Representation', in Arend Lijphart and Bernard Grofman (eds), *Choosing an Electoral System: Issues and Alternatives*, New York: Praeger.

Katz, Richard S. (1986), 'Intraparty Preference Voting', in Bernard Grofman and Arend Lijphart (eds), *Electoral Laws and Their Political Consequences*, New York: Agathon Press.

Katz, Richard S. (1989), 'International Bibliography on Electoral Systems' (revised and expanded edn), *International Political Science Association*, Comparative Representation and Electoral Systems Research Committee.

Katz, Richard S. (1992), 'International Bibliography on Electoral Systems'

(Third Edition), *International Political Science Association*, Comparative Representation and Electoral Systems Research Committee.

Katz, Richard S. (1996), 'Electoral Reform and the Transformation of Party Politics in Italy', *Party Politics* 2: 31–53.

Kelley, Jonathan and Ian McAllister (1983), 'The Electoral Consequences of Gender in Australia', *British Journal of Political Science* 13: 365–77.

Kelley, Jonathan and Ian McAllister (1984), 'Ballot Paper Cues and the Vote in Australia and Britain: Alphabetic Voting, Sex, and Title', *Public Opinion Quarterly* 48: 452–66.

Kellner, Peter (1992), 'The-Devil-You-Know-Factor', *Representation* 31: 10–12.

Kendall, M. G. and A. Stuart (1950), 'The Law of Cubic Proportion in Election Results', *British Journal of Sociology* 1: 183–97.

Laakso, M. (1979), 'Should a Two-and-a-Half Law Replace the Cube Law in British Elections?', *British Journal of Political Science* 9: 355–84.

Laakso, M. and R. Taagepera (1979), 'Effective Number of Parties: A Measure with Application to West Europe', *Comparative Political Studies* 12: 3–27.

Labour Party (1993), *Report of the Working Party on Electoral Systems, 1993*, London: Labour Party.

Lakeman, Enid (1970), *How Democracies Vote: A Study of Majority and Proportional Electoral Systems* (3rd edn), London: Faber and Faber.

Lancaster, Thomas and W. David Patterson (1990), 'Comparative Pork Barrel Politics: Perception from the West German Bundestacy', *Comparative Political Studies* 27: 458–77.

Lane, John C. (1995), 'The Election of Women under Proportional Representation: The Case of Malta', *Democratization* 2: 140–57.

Laver, Michael and Norman Schofield (1991), *Multiparty Government: The Politics of Coalition in Western Europe*, Oxford: Oxford University Press.

Laver, Michael and K. A. Shepsle (1992), 'Election Results and Coalition Possibilities in Ireland', *Irish Political Studies* 7: 57–72.

Lawson, Kay and Colette Ysmal (1992), 'France: The 1988 Presidential Campaign', in Shaun Bowler and David M. Farrell (eds), *Electoral Strategies and Political Marketing*, Basingstoke: Macmillan.

Lijphart, Arend (1984), *Democracies: Patterns of Majoritarian and Consensus Government in Twenty-One Countries*, New Haven, CT: Yale University Press.

Lijphart, Arend (1986), 'Degrees of Proportionality of Proportional Representation Formulas', in Bernard Grofman and Arend Lijphart (1986), *Electoral Laws and Their Political Consequences*, New York: Agathon Press.

Lijphart, Arend (1986a), 'Proportionality by Non-PR Methods: Ethnic Representation in Belgium, Cyprus, Lebanon, New Zealand, West Germany and Zimbabwe', in Bernard Grofman and Arend Lijphart (eds), *Electoral Laws and Their Political Consequences*, New York: Agathon Press.

Lijphart, Arend (1987), 'The Demise of the Last Westminster System? Comments on the Report of New Zealand's Royal Commission on the Electoral System', *Electoral Studies* 6: 97–103.

Lijphart, Arend (1994), *Electoral Systems and Party Systems: A Study of Twenty-Seven Democracies, 1945–1990*, Oxford: Oxford University Press.

Lijphart, Arend (1994a), 'Democracies: Forms, Performance, and Constitutional Engineering', *European Journal of Political Research* 25: 1–17.

Lijphart, Arend and Bernard Grofman (eds) (1984), *Choosing an Electoral System: Issues and Alternatives*, New York: Praeger.

Loosemore, John and Victor J. Hanby (1971), 'The Theoretical Limits of Maximum Distortion: Some Analytic Expressions for Electoral Systems', *British Journal of Political Science* 1: 467–77.

McAllister, Ian (1992), *Political Behaviour: Citizens, Parties and Elites in Australia*, Melbourne: Longman Cheshire.

McAllister, Ian and Toni Makkai (1993), 'Institutions, Society or Protest? Explaining Invalid Votes in Australian Elections', *Electoral Studies* 12: 23–40.

McAllister, Ian and Stephen White (1995), 'Democracy, Political Parties and Party Formation in Post-communist Russia', *Party Politics* 1: 49–72.

McCarthy, Patrick (1992), 'The Referendum of 9 June', in Stephen Hellman and Gianfranco Pasquino (eds), *Italian Politics: A Review: Volume 7*, London: Pinter.

Mackerras, Malcolm (1990), 'Appendix A: Election Results', in Clive Bean, Ian McAllister and John Warhurst (eds), *The Greening of Australian Politics: The 1990 Federal Election*, Melbourne: Longman Cheshire.

Mackerras, Malcolm (1994), 'Reform of New Zealand's Voting System, 1985–1996', *Representation* 32(118): 36–40.

Mackerras, Malcolm (1996), *The Mackerras 1996 Federal Election Guide*, Canberra: Australian Government Publishing Service.

Mackie, Thomas T. and Richard Rose (1991), *The International Almanac of Electoral History* (3rd edn), Basingstoke: Macmillan.

McLean, Iain (1991), 'Forms of Representation and Systems of Voting', in David Held (ed.), *Political Theory Today*, Cambridge: Polity Press.

McLean, Iain (1992), 'Why Does Nobody in Britain Seem to Pay any Attention to Voting Rules?', in Pippa Norris, Ivor Crewe, David Denver and David Broughton (eds), *British Elections and Parties Yearbook 1992*, Hemel Hempstead: Harvester Wheatsheaf.

Mair, Peter (1986), 'Districting Choices under the Single Transferable Vote', in Bernard Grofman and Arend Lijphart (eds), *Electoral Laws and their Political Consequences*, New York: Agathon Press.

Mair, Peter and Michael Laver (1975), 'Proportionality, PR and STV in Ireland', *Political Studies* 23: 491–500.

Marks, Gary and Clive Bean (1992), 'Sources of Electoral Support for Minor Parties: The Case of the Australian Democrats', *Electoral Studies* 11: 311–33.

Marsh, Michael (1985), 'The Voters Decide? Preferential Voting in European List Systems', *European Journal of Political Research* 13: 365–78.

Müller-Rommel, Ferdinand (ed.) (1989), *New Politics in Western Europe: The Rise and Success of Green Parties and Alternative Lists*, Boulder, CO: Westview.

Müller-Rommel, Ferdinand and Geoffrey Pridham (eds) (1991), *Small Parties in Western Europe: Comparative and National Perspectives*, London: Sage.

Niemi, Richard G., Guy Whitten and Mark Franklin (1992), 'Constituency Characteristics, Individual Characteristics and Tactical Voting in the 1987 British General Election', *British Journal of Political Science* 22: 229–54.

Niemi, Richard G., Guy Whitten and Mark Franklin (1993), 'People who Live in Glass Houses: A Response to Evans and Heath's Critique of our Note on Tactical Voting', *British Journal of Political Science* 23: 549–53.

Nohlen, Dieter (1984), 'Changes and Choices in Electoral Systems', in Arend Lijphart and Bernard Grofman (eds), *Choosing an Electoral System: Issues and Alternatives*, New York: Praeger.

Nohlen, Dieter (1989), *Wahlrecht und Parteiensystem*, Opladen: Leske and Budrich.

Norris, Pippa (1994), 'Labour Party Quotas for Women', in David Broughton, David Farrell, David Denver and Colin Rallings (eds), *British Elections and Parties Yearbook, 1994*, London: Frank Cass.

Norris, Pippa (1995), 'The Politics of Electoral Reform in Britain', *International Political Science Review* 16: 65–78.

Norris, Pippa (1995a), 'Introduction: The Politics of Electoral Reform', *International Political Science Review* 16: 3–8.

Norris, Pippa (1996), 'Legislative Recruitment', in Lawrence LeDuc, Richard G. Niemi and Pippa Norris (eds), *Comparing Democracies*, Thousand Oaks, CA: Sage.

Norris, Pippa and Ivor Crewe (1994), 'Did the British Marginals Vanish? Proportionality and Exaggeration in the British Electoral System Revisited', *Electoral Studies* 13(3): 201–21.

Norton, Philip (1993), 'Introduction: Parliament Since 1960', in Mark Franklin and Philip Norton (eds), *Parliamentary Questions*, Oxford: Clarendon Press.

Norton, Philip and D. Wood (1990), 'Constituency Service by Members of Parliament: Does it Contribute to a Personal Vote?', *Parliamentary Affairs* 43: 196–208.

O'Connell, Declan (1983), 'Proportional Representation and Intra-Party Competition in Tasmania and the Republic of Ireland', *Journal of Commonwealth and Comparative Politics* 21: 45–70.

O'Leary, Cornelius (1979), *Irish Elections, 1918–1977: Parties, Voters and Proportional Representation*, Dublin: Gill and Macmillan.

Orttung, Robert W. (1996), 'Duma Elections Bolster Leftist Opposition', *Transition* 23 February: 6–11.

Parker, A. J. (1983), 'Localism and Bailiwicks: The Galway West Constituency in the 1977 General Election', *Proceedings of the Royal Irish Academy* 83: C2, 17–36.

Pattie, Charles, Ed Fieldhouse, Ron Johnston and Andrew Russell (1992), 'A Widening Regional Cleavage in British Voting Behaviour, 1964–87: Preliminary Explorations', in Ivor Crewe, Pippa Norris, David Denver, David Broughton (eds), *British Elections and Parties Yearbook, 1991*, Hemel Hempstead: Harvester Wheatsheaf.

Pattie, Charles, Ron Johnston and Ed Fieldhouse (1993), '*Plus ça change?* The Changing Electoral Geography of Great Britain, 1979–92', in David Denver, Pippa Norris, David Broughton and Colin Rallings (eds), *British Elections and Parties Yearbook, 1993*, Hemel Hempstead: Harvester Wheatsheaf.

Plant, Lord Raymond (1991), *The Plant Report: A Working Party on Electoral Reform*, London: *Guardian* Studies, Volume 3.

Poguntke, Thomas (1994), 'Parties in a Legalistic Culture: The Case of Germany', in Richard S. Katz and Peter Mair (eds), *How Parties Organize: Change and Adaptation in Party Organizations in Western Democracies*, London: Sage.

Poguntke, Thomas, with Bernhard Boll (1992), 'Germany', in Richard S. Katz and Peter Mair (eds), *Party Organizations: A Data Handbook*, London: Sage.

Proportional Representation Society (1919), *Sligo Municipal Elections, 1919: The First Town Council in the United Kingdom Elected by Proportional Representation*, London: Proportional Representation Society (PR Pamphlet No. 41).

Pulzer, Peter (1983), 'Germany', in Vernon Bogdanor and David Butler (eds), *Democracy and Elections: Electoral Systems and Their Political Consequences*, Cambridge: Cambridge University Press.

Punnett, R. M. (1991), 'The Alternative Vote Revisited', *Electoral Studies* 10: 281–98.

Rae, Douglas (1967), *The Political Consequences of Electoral Laws*, New Haven, CT: Yale University Press.

Rallings, Colin (1987), 'The Influence of Election Programs: Britain and Canada, 1945–79', in Ian Budge, David Robertson and D. Hearl (eds), *Ideology, Strategy and Party Change*, Cambridge: Cambridge University Press.

Reeve, Andrew and Alan Ware (1992), *Electoral Systems: A Comparative and Theoretical Introduction*, London: Routledge.

Reynolds, Andrew (1994), 'The Consequences of South Africa's PR Electoral System', *Representation* 32(119): 57–60.

Riker, William H. (1986), 'Duverger's Law Revisited', in Bernard Grofman and Arend Lijphart (eds), *Electoral Laws and Their Political Consequences*, New York: Agathon Press.

Roberts, Geoffrey K. (1975), 'The Federal Republic of Germany', in S. E. Finer (ed.), *Adversary Politics and Electoral Reform*, London: Anthony Wigram.

Roberts, Geoffrey K. (1988) 'The "Second Vote" Campaign Strategy of the West German Free Democratic Party', *European Journal of Political Research* 16: 317–37.

Robson, Christopher and Brendan Walsh (1974), 'The Importance of Positional Voting Bias in the Irish General Election of 1973', *Political Studies* 22: 191–203.

Roche, Richard (1982), 'The High Cost of Complaining Irish Style', *Journal of Irish Business and Administrative Research* 4: 98–108.

Rose, Richard (1980), *Do Parties Make a Difference?*, Chatham, NJ: Chatham House.

Sacks, Paul Martin (1976), *The Donegal Mafia*, New Haven, CT: Yale University Press.

Sartori, Giovanni (1986), 'The Influence of Electoral Systems: Faulty Laws or Faulty Method?', in Bernard Grofman and Arend Lijphart (eds), *Electoral Laws and Their Political Consequences*, New York: Agathon Press.

Sartori, Giovanni (1994), *Comparative Constitutional Engineering: An Inquiry into Structures, Incentives and Outcomes*, Basingstoke: Macmillan.

Schmitt, David E. (1973), *The Irony of Irish Democracy: The Impact of Political Culture on Administrative and Democratic Political Development in Ireland*, Lexington: Lexington Books.

Shiratori, Rei (1995), 'The Politics of Electoral Reform in Japan', *International Political Science Review* 16: 79–94.

Sinnott, Richard (1993), 'The Electoral System', in John Coakley and Michael Gallagher (eds), *Politics in the Republic of Ireland* (2nd edn), Dublin: Folens/PSAI Press.

Sinnott, Richard (1995), *Irish Voters Decide: Voting Behaviour in Elections and Referendums Since 1918*, Manchester: Manchester University Press.

Taagepera, Rein (1990) 'The Baltic States', *Electoral Studies* 9: 303–11.

Taagepera, Rein and Matthew Soberg Shugart (1989), *Seats and Votes: The Effects and Determinants of Electoral Systems*, New Haven, CT: Yale University Press.

Vowles, Jack (1995), 'The Politics of Electoral Reform in New Zealand', *International Political Science Review* 16: 95–115.

Wattenberg, Martin P. (1994), *The Decline of American Political Parties, 1952–1992* (4th edn), Cambridge, MA: Harvard University Press.

Weaver, Leon (1986), 'The Rise, Decline and Resurrection of Proportional Representation in Local Governments in the United States', in Bernard Grofman and Arend Lijphart (eds), *Electoral Laws and their Political Consequences*, New York: Agathon Press.

Weir, Stuart (1992), 'Waiting for Change: Public Opinion and Electoral Reform', *Political Quarterly* 63: 197–221.

Whyte, John (1966), *Dáil Deputies: Their Work, its Difficulties, Possible Remedies*, Dublin: Tuairim Pamphlet No. 15.

Whyte, John (1983), 'How Much Discrimination Was There under the Unionist Regime, 1921–68?', in Tom Gallagher and James O'Connell (eds), *Contemporary Irish Studies*, Manchester: Manchester University Press.

Wilder, Paul (1993), 'The Estonian Elections of 1992: Proportionality and Party Organisation in a New Democracy', *Representation* 31: 72–6.

Wood, Alan H. and Roger Wood (eds) (1992), *The Times Guide to the House of Commons, April 1992*, London: Times Books.

Wright, Jack F. H. (1980), *Mirror of the Nation's Mind: Australia's Electoral Experiments*, Sydney: Hale and Iremonger.

Wright, Jack F. H. (1986), 'Australian Experience with Majority-Preferential and Quota-Preferential Systems', in Bernard Grofman and Arend Lijphart (eds), *Electoral Laws and Their Political Consequences*, New York: Agathon Press.

Ysmal, Colette (1994), 'France', *European Journal of Political Research* 26: 293–304.

Zanella, Remo (1990), 'The Maltese Electoral System and its Distorting Effects', *Electoral Studies* 9: 205–15.

INDEX